T0247931

Who Killed Jules Crevaux?

HAU
Books

Director
Anne-Christine Taylor

Editorial Collective
Erik Bähre
Deborah Durham
Casey High
Nora Scott

Managing Editor
Jane Sabherwal

Hau Books is published by the
Society for Ethnographic Theory (SET)

www.haubooks.org

Who Killed Jules Crevaux?

Murder in the Bolivian Chaco

Isabelle Combès

Preface by Francis Grandhomme

Introduction by Diego Villar

Translated by Nora Scott

HAU Books
Chicago

Initially published as *Qui a tué Jules Crevaux? Le dossier criminel bolivien*

© 2022 Éditions La Valette, French edition
© 2023 Hau Books , English translation

Who Killed Jules Crevaux: Murder in the Bolivian Chaco, by Isabelle Combès

Translated from the French by Nora Scott, Preface by Francis Grandhomme, Introduction by Diego Villar

Cover design: Daniele Meucci
Layout design: Deepak Sharma, Prepress Plus Technologies
Typesetting: Prepress Plus Technologies (https://prepressplustechnologies.com)

ISBN: 978-1-912808-56-4 [Paperback]
LCCN: 2023923544

Hau Books
Chicago Distribution Center
11030 S. Langley Ave.
Chicago, IL 60628
www.haubooks.org

Hau Books publications are marketed, and distributed by The University of Chicago Press.
www.press.uchicago.edu

Printed in the United States of America and the United Kingdom on acid-free paper.

Hau books would like to thank the French Archives nationales for their generous permission to reproduce illustrations contained in this book.

Contents

List of Figures

List of Tables

It was sombre enough, too—and pitiful—not extraordinary in any way—not very clear either. No, not very clear.
Joseph Conrad, *Heart of Darkness*

Some loose ends were painstakingly tied up; others remained unsolved. Many explanations were offered, most of them contradictory. But no one ever managed to answer the most important question.
Henning Mankell, *Firewall*

Preface

Francis Grandhomme

"Who killed Jules Crevaux?" Isabelle Combès rightly asks as she reopens a case thought to have been closed long ago. I say "a case" because we are talking about a crime committed in April 1882. At the time, it captured the attention of both the press and the public: an important scientific expedition disappeared somewhere along the banks of the Rio Pilcomayo, the river marking the border between Bolivia, Argentina, and Paraguay. "An event that will send shock waves through the world," a Buenos Aires newspaper predicted (*Le Courier de la Plata*, May 16, 1882). Because Crevaux wasn't just anyone: he was "one of the greatest explorers of the nineteenth century," declared the Congrès Géographique International de Venise in September 1881, a seasoned traveler and already famous at the age of thirty-five for his three voyages to Guyana, the Amazon basin, and the Orinoco basin, marked by the discovery of the secret of making curare.

The verdict was a foregone conclusion: a man of his stature could only have been undone through treachery; among the many perfect suspects were the fierce Toba Indians of the Chaco, who were the subject of all manner of tales, each more horrific than the last. It is this assumption that Isabelle Combès calls into question.

To understand the Crevaux case and the mystery surrounding it, some context is called for. Crevaux was an explorer and a man of science, but he was not another Paul-Émile Victor or a Jacques Cousteau. In addition to the geographical survey, Jules Crevaux, like his contemporaries, had other specific aims: to open up the remote, unexplored territories, forge pathways, promote trade and colonization, and "civilize" the exotic inhabitants of the area. Even if he was acting as a humanist, even if he publicly deplored the ravages of colonization, the epidemics that decimated the Indian populations, and slavery, he did not question the legitimacy of bringing "civilization"—Western civilization, that goes without saying. As he was about to embark on the waters of the Pilcomayo, a scant few days before his death, he wrote in a Bolivian newspaper: "My thanks to the Franciscan fathers who so effectively aided the cause of Bolivian civilization" by Christianizing and "civilizing" the Indigenous peoples of the Chaco. Crevaux was a "missionary of progress."[1]

Even today, Crevaux's reputation rests on this ambiguity. "Crevaux? The very kind of explorer I avoid," Michel Le Bris provokingly opens his segment on Crevaux in his "dictionary" of explorers, "the kind that immerses himself in the unknown only to destroy it";[2] after this, Le Bris goes on to praise him. It is this ambiguity, too, that would ultimately be the cause of Crevaux's death and above all of the mystery surrounding his disappearance.

Reading *Who Killed Jules Crevaux?*, we realize that, despite the hundreds of pages written about him, we still know very little about the murder of the expedition members. The few studies on the subject are based on often secondary, sometimes deliberately misleading, and always fragmentary French sources. Isabelle Combès, who lives in Bolivia near the site of the massacre, has had the happy idea to conduct her investigation *in situ*, where she seeks out firsthand sources, many of which are unpublished. Her approach is revolutionary.

The reader is plunged less into something like the mystery of the disappearance of Colonel Fawcett, made famous by Peter Flemming in *Brazilian Adventure*, than into the plot of a police investigation worthy of Sherlock Holmes or Arsène Lupin (the famous fictional French housebreaker-turned-detective who lived in Paris at ... 8 rue Crevaux). Or rather into something reminiscent of Mario Vargas Llosa's *Who Killed Palomino Molero?*, unless it's Hitchcock's *The Trouble with Harry*.[3]

As we read, we gradually begin to grasp the true motives for the crime and to understand why it has never been explained. The killing took place somewhere along the disputed border between three South American countries—Bolivia, Argentina, and Paraguay—where Bolivian settlers, Italian missionaries, "subjugated" Indigenous people, and other "savages" regularly clashed. We do not know precisely either the location of the crime, or the circumstances, or even the number of victims, not to mention the killers' names. All persons involved directly or indirectly are immediately contradicted by others. The witnesses end up being suspected of complicity, as are the amateur detectives. Ultimately they turn on each other in self-defense. With time, the uncertainties grow as early firsthand testimony is forgotten. The killing remains wrapped in mystery and entangled in equivocal, erroneous, ambiguous, or contradictory evidence; the Toba people morph into cannibals in the European imagination; Crevaux himself recedes behind his myth.

While it is written and structured like a veritable mystery novel, the present book is nevertheless a true story, which the author situates in its time frame, and its geographical and anthropological contexts. It is also part of a larger body of work. In her earlier publications, such as the *Historia del pérfido Cuñamboy* (2016), Isabelle Combès adopts a viewpoint that includes the Indigenous populations (at the time of the Crevaux affair, any defense they may have advanced left no trace). And if she speaks of "faceless killers" (perhaps a reference to one of Henning Mankell's novels),[4] she attempts to give a face to these Indigenous people, much like an attorney for the defense. She is thus not proposing a simple change of scenery, but a journey through a forgotten story, in an excellent investigation with a distinctly literary resonance.

So why should this criminal case be revisited?

Because it offers scope for a novel.

Even if everything is true.

Or could be …

Francis Grandhomme
CRULH-Nancy EA39-45
Lycée Fustel de Coulanges-Strasbourg

Introduction

The Seventh Circle (in the Chaco), or Murder Considered as a Method

Diego Villar

As the pathologist in a detective novel might say, standing before a body that is still warm—I'm thinking here of Max DeBryn, or perhaps of the short-tempered Dr. Pasquano—a few facts are clear. We know, for instance, that the renowned explorer Jules Crevaux, "the South American Livingstone" who had just successfully crossed Guyana, the Amazon, and the Orinoco, was murdered along the Pilcomayo River on April 27, 1892. Just a few days into their journey, the party of five Frenchmen, two Argentinians, nine Bolivians, and a native interpreter was attacked by an unknown Indigenous group, resulting in the death of several expedition members. The description of the scenery is also apparently clear: the drama unfolds in an area of the Bolivian Chaco claimed at the time by both Argentina and Paraguay. These young republics were seeking to consolidate their presence in a region which was largely Indigenous territory, while the liberal governments of Bolivia were desperately organizing expeditions to secure some sort of access to the sea. Meanwhile a series of secularizing policies was antagonizing the religious missions that had spearheaded regional colonization, the Indigenous communities were migrating en masse to the northwest of Argentina to grasp the favorable opportunities for work, and the various ethnic groups in the Chaco were coming to realize that they needed to join forces in the struggle against

1

the whiteman. In such a volatile situation, it is no wonder that the smallest spark could provoke violence, and indeed the general turmoil in the Chaco presented—in the words of one of the privileged witnesses of the time—"an Iliad of sins, crimes and scandals, revenge, cruelty, outrages, thefts, arrogance, and the law of might makes right."[1]

The chaotic nature of the scenario, which at first sight could be attributed to the general situation or to the very ambiguities of the colonization process, was not, however, the only factor complicating the external perception of a region like the Chaco—described from the very outset as a space of miscegenation, trade, multiculturalism, and multilingualism, where "everything is mixture"[2] and the principles of political, economic, or social organization that define other cultural areas of Amerindian ethnology are not clearly drawn.[3] In this regard, at least from the external point of view, the uncertainty, chaos, and general turmoil are by no means accidents but are in the very nature of the region. They are not things that happen in the Chaco; they *are* the Chaco. The murder of Crevaux in 1892 goes some way to reinforcing this perception. The tragedy provoked as much shock in Bolivia as it did in Argentina and France, home of the expeditionary party; but as the detective/ethnohistorian Isabelle Combès remarks, the actual murder is in fact the only reliable information we have. The general commotion prompted by the Crevaux myth is a vanishing trail of rumors, legends, snippets of information, forgetfulness, misunderstandings, half-truths, lies, opacities, exaggerations, and even blatant falsifications.[4] In a plot in which nothing can be assumed to be true, all versions are to a certain degree plausible, the actors are both victims and detectives, and everyone—Indigenous peoples, explorers, colonists, military men, missionaries, guides, interpreters, cooks, witnesses—accuses everyone else: just as in detective novels, the suspense is maintained by suggesting at every step that the culprit is someone else.

The very uncertainties that infuriate the ethnologist or the historian are sure to delight the reader of the detective genre. Behind this choice, however, I glimpse something more than mere literary affinity. Timidly the author claims that the only common denominator behind the tangle of conflicting pieces of information, opacities, and nonsense involved in the Crevaux myth is that, each in his own way, the explorers present themselves as icons of civilization and progress. The narrative trope is undoubtedly correct but it seems insufficient, which is why I would venture a little further. In this sense, the decision to choose the detective format is not exactly innocent. Let us recall that, for a reflexive practitioner of the detective story, such as Jorge Luis Borges, the genre is equivalent to functional architecture or figurative painting.[5] In other words, unlike free verse, impressionist painting, or the sentimental novel, it is a genre that avoids chaos and owes its efficacy—frequently outstandingly popular— to the fact that it preserves a set of classical virtues: identifiable characters, fixed rules, logical order, elements adapted to produce a certain effect, and a structure with a beginning, development, and conclusion. In other words, the unexpressed goal of a long line of descent stretching from Poe to Chesterton and Bustos Domecq, or from Holmes's heroin injections to Morse's glasses of ale and whisky, and even Wallander's Alzheimer's, would be to preserve the illusion of order in times of chaos. In Borges, but also in the works of a group of intellectuals from the first half of the twentieth century who orbited around him (Bioy Casares, Manuel Peyrou, the Ocampo sisters), there was in fact a pedagogical and political decision to promote the detective genre as a tool to foster rational thought: an ideal of playing by the rules but, at the same time, a critical apparatus accessible to all, designed to manage chaos in an era of mechanical reproduction of irrationalism, propaganda, and fraud.[6]

Therefore, venturing beyond the stated intentions of Combès, the heuristic invitation to take the detective novel as a beacon may shed light on the latent spirit of the inquiry. Beyond the charm of the plot, as in the adventures of hairdresser Isidro Parodi, Father Brown, or Auguste Dupin, what we can take from this book is basically a lesson in method that, like the best of them, slips surreptitiously into the reader's conscience. With the days of the evolutionist anthropologies, of the tales of *Naturvölker*, or the tidy typologies of the *Handbook of South American Indians* long gone, we are now well aware that nobody continues to claim that the Indigenous peoples of South American are or were "people without a history" or "cold societies" frozen in time and reluctant to change.[7] What is not so clear is the very nature of this "temporal revolution" and the precise relationship of those societies, and their specific regimes of historicity, and the diachronic processes.[8]

This is where, I believe, this book makes a contribution. When academics speak of "ethnohistory" they generally refer to a series of problems defined by a more-or-less canonical historiographic agenda, recorded in places where there happened to be Indigenous peoples: the missions at X, the frontier Y, the impact of this or that reform in Z.[9] The gaze is focused on the "process," and it is basically immaterial whether it involves the Toba, Tapiete, Wichí, or Nivaclé. This book, on the other hand, aims to forge a true historical anthropology, or perhaps an ethnohistory in which the stress clearly lies on the prefix "ethno": a narrative that rewrites the Indigenous version of the event by following a logic that eludes the designs of governments, functionaries, scientific societies, religious orders, social classes, and armies—not because the rigors of the academic modes or political correctness of the day require it, but because it is a history in an Indigenous key.[10]

First, in this type of analysis it does definitely matter whether those who killed Crevaux were Tobas, Chiriguanos, or Wichís: in fact, each of the groups and factions that compose those ethnic labels has their own particularities, and it is not at all the same whether Crevaux was shot, stabbed, drowned, or scalped. Second, Indigenous peoples are viewed in all cases as actual protagonists, and not secondary figures or supporting actors in great processes they are unable to fully appreciate or understand. Third and perhaps most important, they are protagonists who have followed their own agenda—as practical or idealistic as any other—and not icons, emblems, or allegories of something else: resistance to colonization, economic marginality, ethnicity, ecology, ontology, Indigenous metaphysics. Much to the despair of observers, the Indigenous actors are, in fact, often unperturbed about presenting their voices or points of view as testimonies, or about presenting themselves as victims, or as spokespersons for any idea, culture, or community; this is simply because they are not just mere embodied political positions, epistemologies, or ecologies. And this is precisely what makes them credible: the fact that they are persons driving forward their own agenda, to mediate, negotiate, consolidate prestige or power, avenge an offence, seize opportunities, defend a territory, survive. As powerful as the network of influences spreading through the marginality of the Chaco may be, the "white world" was also being transformed by the actions of Yallá, Yahuanahua, Calaeta, Catuna, Calisin, Cuserai, Pelocolic, Caligagae, Iñiri, Cutaicoliqui, Socó, Cototo, El Rengo, Mandepora, Autagaicoluqui, Cutiguasu, Iramaye, Chiriqui, Oleoncito, Icuru, Blanco, or Tatuyuruy. According to Combès, the decisions, strategies, and even the whims of each one of them has as much thematic weight as those of the French explorers, Argentinian military men, or Italian missionaries. Their motivations—surely multicausal—are appreciated in much the same way as the classical historian assesses the official policy of colonization of a hitherto savage frontier. It is thus not a question of vindicating or criticizing this or that action by characters such as Ibarreta, Thouar, or Crevaux himself, in which the Tobas or the Chiriguanos incidentally appear; it is the fact that the travelers, functionaries, soldiers, missionaries, and even national and international heroes—whatever fame they may have garnered in the Société de Géographie in Paris—appear as supporting actors in the bizarre "Far West" of the Chaco, and even end up dying for some obscure reason they never know: revenge, the kidnapping of a woman, the ill humor of this or that native leader, failed diplomacy, or a setback in a petty exchange.

Her intention to rewrite regional and national history in Indigenous code was already present in works such as *Etno-historias del Isoso*, in which Combès analyzes centuries of micropolitics by Chané and Chiriguano leaders in the foothills of the Andes. Far from following a consistent political strategy over the years, the leaders manipulated the Indigenous inhabitants (both the Guarani-speaking factions and the groups of Chaco ancestry), the various colonizing agents (*encomienda* authorities, explorers, missionaries, military men, naturalists) and also the republican actors (settlers, farmers, livestock breeders, sugar-mill owners, national armies, functionaries, and, nowadays, NGOs, anthropologists, and development projects).

Combès's methodological inflection took a deeper step in the exemplary biography of Cuñamboy, a Chiriguano leader, *Historia del pérfido Cuñamboy*, which reveals at a personal level the game of fleeting loyalties.[11] The son of Captain Maruama, Santiago Cuñamboy was baptized in a Franciscan mission and from an early age took part in expeditions to suppress the Chiriguano rebellions, for which the Spanish authorities praised his bravery. But over the years, his affiliations became much more problematic, unstable, and fluid. These were the days of the Plan Viedma, which, against the backdrop of the Bourbon reforms, sought to secularize the missions of the so-called Cordillera Chiriguana: the aim was to end the Franciscan protection of the Indians and open the missions to regional commerce. Franciscans, colonists, and military men accused each other of exploiting the Indigenous peoples, mistreating them, and abusing their womenfolk. On inheriting his father's position, Cuñamboy publicly denounced the exploitation of the military, to such an extent that they accused him of being an agent of the missions, dismissed him, and sentenced him to the stocks. However he then accused the priests of a series of sexual abuses. Then, at the end of the eighteenth century, new Indigenous rebellions broke out, and the Spanish accused Cuñamboy of inciting them. But in 1804, the official chronicles show him accompanying the Spanish military again. In fact both the priests and the military are pieces on the checkerboard of an internal confrontation between Cuñamboy and another Chiriguano cacique, Potica.

With the wars of independence, Cuñamboy's position became more ambiguous than ever. In 1813, Manuel Belgrano led the army of Alto

Perú out of Potosí to fight the royalist troops. The patriotic general was assisted by the powerful Captain, Cumbay: however, an analysis of the correspondence of the time reveals the constant problems between the independence forces and their Chiriguano allies—one of whom was obviously Cuñamboy, who wasted no time in changing sides. He then appears to conspire with the Franciscans against the military, but what actually interested him was his new confrontation with the Indigenous leader, Pedro Guariyu. Cuñamboy staged an attempted coup, and everything seems to indicate that he died at the hands of the patriotic troops.

So it is clear that separating the "patriotic Chiriguanos" from the "royalist Chiriguanos" lacks any diagnostic value. Firstly because the "royalists" seem to be concerned with the fate of the Franciscan friars rather than with the distant and abstract cause of the King; secondly because a character such as Cuñamboy changes sides as a matter of expediency (for instance, his confrontation with Guariyu); thirdly, to complicate matters even further, because "barbaric" or "savage" Indigenous fighters, for whom the differences between supporters of the Crown or supporters of independence are of little importance, also appear in the Cordillera, seeking to make the most of the continental confrontation to rid themselves of all the *karai* (whitemen).

Perhaps the crux of the problem is having supposed that the Indigenous captains represented the Chiriguano "ethnic group" or "people" as a homogeneous body, when everything seems to indicate they were in fact fighting over the leadership of the local and regional captaincies, and the alliances with traders, missionaries, patriots, and royalists were means to shift the regional balances of power in their favor.[12] Cuñamboy sided with the Franciscans to defeat Potica but then had no qualms about denouncing those very same priests that were his former allies. Similarly, for a period he sided with the royalist band in the war of independence but then joined the patriots and those Chiriguanos who sympathized with neither one band nor the other. His aim was to regain his former freedom—and he does so, now to counteract the growing power of a new Indigenous competitor. The idea of understanding things from the Indigenous point of view reappears here in full: if external agents sought to use him for their own interests, it is clear that Cuñamboy also used them to settle internal disagreements in the communities and to dispatch possible rivals for power. Far from genuinely involving himself in the conflicts between Indigenous peoples and whitemen, missionaries, patriots, and royalist armies, Cuñamboy used each situation to promote his own agenda. From this point of view, there is no possible ambiguity since he was always on the same side: that of Cuñamboy. What is most important is that, from that angle, the lability of the character is not seen as a means to give local color to the historical study of the independence process, but that the war of independence becomes just another instrument to shed light on the biography of an extraordinary Indigenous leader.

The analytic possibility of using documentary scaffolding to recreate the points of view of Cuñamboy, Yallá, or Cutaicoliqui, and to highlight and prioritize such a perspective over other historical processes—whether they be the Bourbon reforms, the wars of independence, the rise of extractivism, the Chaco War, or decolonization—is not only a question of scale (bringing the lens nearer and focusing on the daily minutiae of local microhistory), but a question of profoundly transforming historiography in search of a new experience that is more ethnographic, more symmetrical, and less extractive.[13] This form of understanding South American history not only allows Combès to write a history in Indigenous code of the same spaces that traditional historiography views as "deserts," "contact zones," "peripheries," or "frontiers," but it additionally allows her to calibrate in a novel fashion the different interfaces and relationships between the local and the global, between external influence and internal adaptation.

That is exactly why this type of analysis offers us a point of equilibrium between two interpretive ideal types, between which the ethnology and the history of the South American lowlands usually alternate. On the one hand, we have those studies that understand the Indigenous peoples (or Creoles or peasants) as mere marginal or subordinate actors whose existence is diluted in the web of external decisions made by the state, national culture, missions, armies, extractive industries, or development projects. From this point of view, there is no real difference between a Wichí from the northern Chaco or a Mapuche from the south of Chile, because what matters is that both are oppressed, invisibilized, or marginalized in a more-or-less passive subordination to capitalism, to religious indoctrination, or to extractivism. On the other hand, we find an exacerbated multiculturalism whose only interest seems to be to trace the semantic, symbolic, and epistemological consistency of the native systems of action and thought: from this perspective, anything that comes from "outside" ends up being absorbed and recycled in culturally acceptable terms, and there is no substantial difference between minor Pentecostal devotion or the Catholic Church, an abusive boss or a national army, a small-scale farmer or Monsanto, since ultimately everything is swallowed up by an all-powerful hyperagency. Against the first interpretative apparatus, the historical anthropology proposed by Combès suggests that archival work can reveal that the millennialism that drove the Guaycurú revolts had in fact a transfigured cosmological matrix of Tupí-Guaraní origin. Against the second, we realize that the "anti-colonial" resistance of those Guaranís whose culture permeated the north of the Chaco and the foothills of the Andes was not an instance of nebulous metaphysics "against the state," and that cultural framework combined in sui generis fashion with the strategic search for power and legitimacy.[14]

On clearing away over the years the tangle of opaque factors, complex motives, and impossible names, Combès dismantles an opposition that is sitting too comfortably and too easily between—if I may use the Nordenskiöldian expression—"Indians and white men," and exposes with an almost manic (or detective-like) patience the multiple forms in which one can track the realignment between the fractures in the diverse *karai* factions (missionaries and settlers, patriots and royalists, liberals and conservatives, Frenchmen, Argentinians, and Bolivians) and Indigenous peoples (Chiriguano and Toba, Wichí and Nivaclé, Potica and Cuñamboy, Cuñamboy and Pedro Guariyu). That is not bad for a book which, after all, offers no more than conundrums, including that of its own genre. We will never know who, where, or how Crevaux was actually murdered; nor will we know if the work that offers the rationale for his murder is a police novel, a historical novel, a history book, an ethnohistory, or an ethnography. What we will know is that it is an enjoyable read and that it is clearly good anthropology—especially if we bear in mind that someone once said that anthropology is either historical, or it is nothing.[15]

Acknowledgments

This text is part of the Horizon Europe research and innovation program under the Marie Sklodowska-Curie GA 101060942.

Diego Villar
Università Ca' Foscari Venezia

Who Killed Jules Crevaux?

CHAPTER I

Reopening the File

The Detective Speaks

I would willingly subscribe to the term "decolonizing history," were it not so often misused and pressed into the service of political ideologies of the moment in too many countries, my own place of residence, Bolivia, included. To decolonize history all too often comes down to simply inverting the poles: there where the nineteenth century, or later Hollywood, lauded the brave settlers bringing progress, today we find merciless, cruel conquerors; there where the colonial governments saw barely human savages, today we are given innocent victims and civilizations ravaged by the West. Even if a change of perspective is salutary and not lacking in truth, history continues to be told in black and white; it is still conceived as an overly simple narrative opposing good and evil, without shading, without the gray areas that, ultimately, define the complexity of real life. It remains a story without a history.

That is why I find no term to describe what I have set out to do, unless it is simply to write a plural historical anthropology, which gives a place to the different facets and the various figures without favoring any one over the others. According to the "colonial version," a hundred and forty years ago, an unexplained crime was committed somewhere in a forgotten hinterland of Latin America: Jules Crevaux died in Bolivia at the hands of Indians[1] in the Chaco. His killing caused a stir. The world lamented the sad fate of the brave victim fallen into the hands of cruel savages. Crevaux became an icon, an emblem of civilization and progress, fallen like a martyr under the blows of barbarism. In all wars, however, martyrs serve a cause, and avenging Crevaux became yet one more pretext to bolster the colonization of a rebellious region.

As in any good inquest, and given the celebrity of the explorer, the extant literature was interested in the victim's personality. The crime became the "Crevaux affair," although some fifteen other men died with him: French, but also Argentinians, and Bolivians. What were they doing there? Is their death any less important because they were not known? Who was interested in the killers' motives? Their savagery, their "natural" cruelty were enough to explain the killing, no need to look any farther. The result was a story the like of those found in the Tintin comic books, with the Good Guys and the Bad Guys, the hero and the rest.

To "decolonize" this story would mean reversing the perspective and showing that the guilty parties—the Amerindians—were merely defending their territories and their freedom. And all that is true. But it is also true that the story is much richer, much more complex. In this version, the Indians turn on each other rather than uniting to fight the invader; the colonial agents—missionaries and settlers—are busy fighting among themselves rather than subjugating the Indigenous populations. The mystery that arose around Crevaux's death stems precisely from these accusations and counteraccusations, from these diverging interests, which did not retain the attention of the various authors, focused as they were on the figure of Crevaux.

In the following pages, then, I propose a historical approach to anthropology, taking, as the pretext and narrative thread, the murder of the members of the Crevaux expedition. In order to shed light (or at least a bit more light) on this crime, such an approach must consider the whole set of forces and how they play out; this historical essay must therefore search out the original documents, left to gather dust in the Bolivian archives and lie unconsulted, as though the history of the Indians were not also inscribed in the archives or as though everything had already been said. The story of Crevaux's death is also the story of the conquest of one of the last unsubjugated territories in South America, and investigating the crime reveals the hidden or little-known mechanisms, and makes known the different protagonists, whose names are not contained in the history books but all of whom have helped write an unacknowledged page of the Indigenous history of the Gran Chaco and of Bolivia itself. *Cui bono?* Who gains from the crime? That is the question we must answer. But as in any self-respecting mystery novel, it is too early to reveal the solution.

Persons Involved

The French
JULES CREVAUX, French naval physician and explorer
JOSEPH DIDELOT, alias Jean-François Payeur, Crevaux's secretary
ERNEST HAURAT, helmsman for the Crevaux expedition
THÉOPHILE NOVIS, Alsatian artist, accompanied Thouar on the 1887 expedition
ARTHUR THOUAR, explorer, followed in the footsteps of the Crevaux expedition in 1883, led a new expedition in 1887

The Bolivian Criollos
GUMERCINDO ARANCIBIA, military physician, head of the Crevaux military settlement in 1883
MARTÍN BARROSO, settler and landowner
DANIEL CAMPOS, Bolivian government delegate and leader of an expedition to the Pilcomayo River basin in 1883
JOSÉ NAPOLEÓN CORREA, captured by the Tobas in childhood and freed in 1884
CECILIA OVIEDO, young wife of a settler-soldier, captured by the Tobas in 1884
EUDOGIO RAÑA, subprefect of Gran Chaco Province
ANDRÉS RIVAS, soldier and leader of an expedition to the Pilcomayo River basin in 1882
FRANCISCO ZEBALLOS, a surviving member of the Crevaux expedition

The Italians
DOROTEO GIANNECCHINI, Franciscan friar, superior of the Chaco missions
VINCENTE MARCELLETI, Franciscan friar, in charge of the San Antonio Mission in the Pilcomayo River basin

The Indigenous groups
Spelling of Indigenous names varies considerably with the author cited. We have indicated the most frequent spellings. The text reflects the spelling found in the document being cited.

The Chiriguanos (Tupí-Guarani language family)
IRAMAYE, neophyte of the Tigüipa mission, interpreter for the Crevaux mission, massacre survivor

YAHUANAHUA, sent in search of the Crevaux mission by the Yacuiba settlers

The Tobas (Guaykuru language family)
CALIGAGAE, CALICAGAI, Toba leader, father of Yallá
COTOTO, Chiriguano-Toba mestizo, known for his opposition to the missionaries
CUSERAI, CUSERAI, CASERAI, CUZARAY, rebel from the San Francisco mission and sworn enemy of the settlers and missionaries
CUTAICOLIQUI, COTAICOLIQUI, TAICOLIQUI, TAICORIQUE, Toba leader
IÑIRI, YÑIRI, Toba leader
PELOCO, PELOCOLIQUI, PELOCOLIC, PELOKOLIKI, PELOKO, Toba leader, already elderly at the time of the events
PELOCOLIQUI-GUASU, PELOCOLIQUI-GUAZU, PELOCOLIJIGUASU, Toba leader, probably Peloco's son
SOCÓ, Cototo's brother, also hostile to the missionaries
YALLÁ, also known as Petrona in Spanish, Caligagae's daughter, captured at Tarija and freed in order to facilitate the arrival of the Crevaux expedition

The Güisnays (Mataco-Mataguayo language family)
SIROME, SILOMI, leader of the Güisnays, living at Piquirenda

Other Indigenous groups
The Noctenes, Notenes or Matacos, belonging to the Mataco-Mataguayo linguistic family
The Chorotes or Chorotis belonging to the Mataco-Mataguayo linguistic family

Important places
The Franciscan missions
MACHARETI, Chiriguano mission
SAN ANTONIO DE PADUA, Noctene mission, on the right bank of the Pilcomayo
SAN FRANCISCO SOLANO, Toba mission, on the left bank of the Pilcomayo
TARAIRI, Chiriguano mission

Military forts and settlements
BELLA ESPERANZA, fort founded on the Pilcomayo by Andrés Rivas in 1863

CREVAUX SETTLEMENT, founded at Teyu on the Pilcomayo, in 1883, by Daniel Campos

Bolivian towns and villages
CAIZA, first village founded by Bolivian settlers, in 1843, near the Pilcomayo
ITIYURU, Bolivian settlement south of Yacuiba
TARIJA, capital of the department of Tarija in the south of Bolivia, location of the Franciscan high school
YACUIBA, large town south of Caiza

Indian camps
CABAYUREPOTI, Toba camp downriver from Teyu
PIQUIRENDA, Güisnay camp, well downriver from Cabayurepoti
TEYU, Toba camp, called Santa Bárbara de Teyu by settlers, downriver from the San Francisco mission on the left bank of the Pilcomayo

The Facts

On April 27, 1882, a young French explorer, Jules Crevaux, and his companions were killed by Indians on the banks of the Pilcomayo River in Bolivia's Gran Chaco. The news sparked strong emotions in both Bolivia and Argentina (Crevaux's access to Bolivia), and of course in France. The international scientific community was in shock.

Born in 1847 at Lorquin in the French department of Lorraine, Jules Crevaux distinguished himself in the 1870 Franco-Prussian war, in the wake of which his home village was annexed by Germany. Crevaux chose France and continued his naval career as a physician; in 1876 he undertook a series of voyages to explore rivers in Guyana, the Amazon River basin, and the Orinoco. This experience confirmed his status as an explorer, and by the time of his death at the age of thirty-five, he was already famous. The first biographies quickly arrived, the earliest scarcely two months after his death. Numerous articles appeared in the geographical reviews, and, a year after the massacre, a posthumous book by the explorer came out, entitled *Voyages en Amérique du Sud*. Biography soon gave way to hagiography, though, and the myth of Jules Crevaux began to take shape: martyr to science, "barefoot explorer," "beggar of Eldorado," "South America's Livingstone."[2] But even if his fame renders

Figure 1. Jules Crevaux
Calling card of J. Crevaux, recto, private archives of Virginio Lema, Tarija.

the emotion sparked by his murder understandable, it only explains it in part: his sudden and tragic death, never really cleared up, casts him as a martyr and the center of an unsolved riddle which greatly contributed to his celebrity.

The only thing we know with any certainty is that the explorer died in 1882 at the hands of Indians, somewhere on the Pilcomayo River, downstream from the Franciscan mission of San Francisco Solano (today Villamontes), and not far from the place where, a year after the crime, the military settlement bearing his name was founded. The rest is wrapped in a skein of mystery and a complex web of vague, equivocal, erroneous, ambiguous, or contradictory information. Crevaux died (but some claim that he survived) somewhere, at an uncertain date and time, killed by anonymous Indians acting perhaps alone or perhaps not, together with an undetermined number of other victims and as many survivors. None of these points has yet to receive a satisfactory, clear, and, especially, unequivocal clarification. All of the presumed witnesses or persons closely, or less closely, involved in Crevaux's exploration were immediately contradicted by others. Doubts ranged from the serious question of the identity of the killers or their motives to such trivial and insignificant details as the time of death (10 a.m., noon, dusk). Ultimately the witnesses were suspected of complicity as were the amateur detectives. All, as I have said, ended up turning on the others in self-defense.

The story unfolds along a vague local border site that was the scene of chronic clashes. Three states (Bolivia, Argentina, and Paraguay) disputed ownership of the *Chaco Boreal* and the banks of the Pilcomayo, though none actually maintained a presence in the region.

The main risk facing a potential detective was to wind up like the victims and be murdered by unsubjugated Indigenous people. Gathering the most important information and clues after Crevaux's death was possible only because the Indians, in other words the main suspects, made it so. This initial information was used in turn to fan the flames in this borderland far from the centers of government, where the state's presence was practically nonexistent and where fierce rivalry prevailed between settlers and Franciscan brothers. Crevaux's death acted as a catalyst, laying bare the secret mechanisms of the remote frontier world and revealing the ambiguous relations among the actors present. It also contributed to intensify the colonization of a hitherto Indian, and solely Indian, region.

The result was that all of the ingredients were present for Crevaux's death to remain a mystery. The confusions and ambiguities were repeated

Figure 2. The Pilcomayo River
Teófilo Novis, *El Chaco en imágenes* ([1887] 2016), p. 116.

or amplified in later writings, thus increasing the uncertainty and giving rise to outright scams and to ill-concealed lies. The "Crevaux myth" was not only that of the devoted explorer, it was also, or above all, that of his death, of his bloodthirsty killers, and of the circumstances of the expedition's massacre.

To immerse oneself in the police investigation of the time, or to venture to reopen it today, is to enter the realm of the fantastic and the unreal, to slide around on slippery ground, to remain wrapped in a fog which dissolves even the most solid evidence. The task entails a double role, of both detective and historian, which are not all that different if the truth be told. The detective must go back over the evidence, clues, testimonies, denunciations, and accusations, in an attempt to determine "what happened." But the tracks have been erased, and we are not allowed to cross-examine the suspects. We are thus left with too many questions without answers, or with too many answers. The modern literature on Crevaux is based on a handful of contemporary writings that we owe to persons directly involved, who acted as detectives, who accused or were themselves accused. These writings in turn have their own sources which must be examined, leaving us with a hodgepodge of unreliable clues, improbable witnesses, and by no means hard-and-fast proofs.

We mustn't have too many illusions: Crevaux's death will largely remain a mystery. In re-creating the climate and the atmosphere of the Chaco frontier at the time, I wanted to understand how so much contradictory information could have arisen and stirred up a whirlwind of accusations from all sides. The main protagonists of this story are not Jules Crevaux or his unfortunate companions. They are the Bolivian settlers, Italian missionaries, Chaco Indians, and explorers of all stripe. It was the relentless colonization of the Chaco that pressed the death of the "martyr to science" into its service. The personality of the victim, or rather victims, is of little import. Crevaux and his companions were not killed for who they were but for what they represented, and for the ideals they embodied.

The Crime Scene

By the beginning of the 1880s, Bolivia had already all but lost its coastline in the Pacific war that opposed it to Chile. To end this confinement, hopes turned to the Atlantic and access to the ocean via the Amazon River basin or the Rio de la Plata. In the latter context, the natural route,

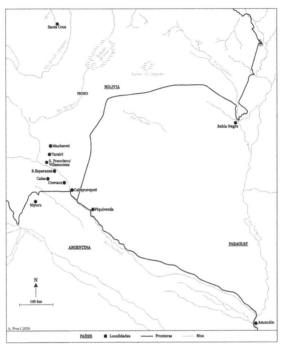

Figure 3. The Chaco Boreal: Principal places mentioned
Drawing by Alberto Preci.

though relatively little known at this *fin de siècle*, was the Pilcomayo River. This waterway rises in the Bolivian Andes (Potosi Department) and flows southeastward, through the departments of Potosi, Chuquisaca, and Tarija. In the last department, at the level of the present-day city of Villamontes (former Franciscan mission of San Francisco Solano), it enters the Gran Chaco plain, flowing in a southwesterly direction to finally join with the Paraguay River slightly downstream from Asunción. The Pilcomayo customarily marks the border between the northern Chaco Boreal (on the left bank) and the Chaco Central to the south (right bank). The Chaco Central in turn is delimited on the south by the other major tributary of the Paraguay, the Bermejo River.

The idea of crossing the Chaco to reach the Paraguay and, from there, the Atlantic Ocean was an old, never-realized dream dating back to the sixteenth century. Whether because of the Indians' fierce resistance or the barriers thrown up by an extremely hostile, dry environment, the Chaco Boreal remained exempt for the duration of the colonial period from exploration and Spain's attempts at settlement. The latter were renewed only during the first century of Bolivia's independence and initially under the government of José Ballivián (1841–1847), who strongly promoted a policy of opening up the country's eastern lowlands.

The Bolivian authorities envisaged two possible routes: one via the Parapeti River, starting from the region of Isoso (Cordillera Province of Santa Cruz Department) and eastward through the Chaco to the Paraguay; the other, which interests us here, via the Pilcomayo, descending the river by boat or following its banks down to Asunción. Before 1882, Bolivia launched several expeditions to explore the Pilcomayo:

- the 1843–1844 expedition led by Manuel Rodríguez Magariños
- the 1844 expedition led by Enrique van Nivel
- the 1863 expedition led by Andrés Rivas, accompanied by the Franciscan, José Gianelli
- and the 1867 expedition led by Sebastián Cainzo

None reached its goal, and almost all (with the exception of the 1863 expedition) were attacked at one time or another by the Indians. This hostility and the natural barriers are the main reasons the explorers were forced to turn back well before they reached the Paraguay. In 1863, the Rivas/Gianelli expedition got no farther than Piquirenda, as far as anyone had reached until then. Nevertheless, added to the expansion of the Franciscan missions of Tarija College at the same time, these explorations gradually augmented the presence of Bolivian *Criollos*[3] in a region that had, until thus far, for all practical purposes evaded state control. In 1843, Magariños founded the military settlement of Villa Rodrigo in the previously Indigenous (Chiriguano) village of Caiza, spearheading the colonization of the Bolivian Chaco. Twenty years later, the Rivas/Gianelli expedition established Fort Bella Esperanza in Tariguiti, on the banks of the Pilcomayo.

Loss of access to the sea at the start of the 1880s encouraged Bolivia to organize new exploratory expeditions to the Pilcomayo. The big unknown was the river's navigability—that was what the Crevaux mission was supposed to ascertain. The question was finally settled in 1892, by Olaf Storm. But even if Bolivia's goal was to discover and exploit a new trade route to remedy its lack of access to the sea, other interests were also at stake. The Pilcomayo, and with it a large portion of the Gran Chaco, were at the center of an international dispute among three neighboring countries: Bolivia, Argentina, and Paraguay. In fact, Argentina, too, was very interested in the Pilcomayo and sponsored several expeditions to the Chaco Boreal in the second half of the nineteenth century.

In 1878, after the War of the Triple Alliance (Brazil, Argentina, and Uruguay) against Paraguay, the verdict of US President Rutherford B. Hayes fixed the course of the Pilcomayo as the international border between Paraguay (to the north, left bank) and Argentina (to the south, right bank). But these accords left the border between Paraguay and Bolivia, and the two countries' claims to the Chaco Boreal in general and the Pilcomayo in particular, up in the air, or at least vague. The border between Bolivia and Argentina was fixed only in 1889 (the Quirno Costas/Vaca Guzmán Treaty), with parallel 22°S as the limit. But Bolivia and Paraguay continued to dispute the Chaco Boreal, and, despite no fewer than five treaties concluded between the two countries between 1879 and 1913, their relations worsened in the following decades, culminating in the Chaco War of 1932–1935.

It was in this rather chaotic, tense, and, for Bolivia, highly constraining, landscape that, in April 1882, Jules Crevaux led his expedition on the Pilcomayo River. In Tarija, the Bolivian government was preparing a new expedition to the Pilcomayo and, to this end, had organized a "Promoting Commission."

Crevaux arrived in Buenos Aires at the end of 1881 with four fellow countrymen. His first aim seems not to have been to explore the Pilcomayo, but rather a much more ambitious project: to travel the Paraguay River upstream to its source and from there embark on a tributary of the Amazon in order to reach the great river. In other terms, the plan was to connect the Amazon and the Rio de la Plata basins. But the explorer changed his mind in Buenos Aires and decided to explore the Pilcomayo, and more specifically to discover whether or not it was navigable.

The decision seems to have been influenced by certain Bolivians, such as the diplomats Modesto Omiste and Vaca Guzmán—the latter extremely interested in the search for an Atlantic route and author of a book on the Pilcomayo, which he gave Crevaux to read. But the Argentinians were also interested in the project and encouraged Crevaux. Whatever the truth may be, Crevaux decided to leave for Tarija. His expedition was sponsored by three countries: France, Argentina (which delegated two naval officers to accompany him and provided, among other things, nineteen good Remington rifles), and Bolivia, which saw to the preparations. The crew that finally embarked on the Pilcomayo was composed of representatives of those three nations.

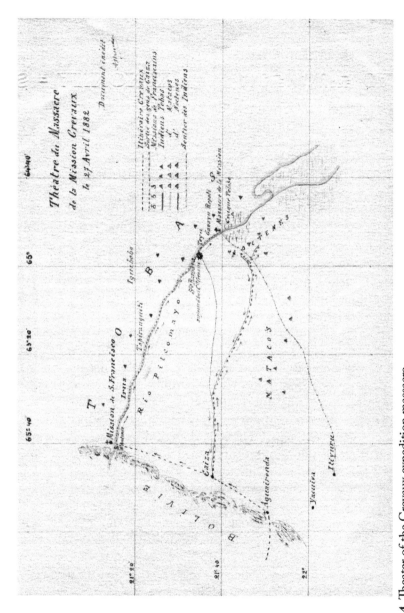

Figure 4. Theater of the Crevaux expedition massacre
Unpublished map by Arthur Thouar (Archives Nationales, F/17/3009B, dossier Thouar).

Crevaux reached Tarija and quickly moved to gather all information possible in view of organizing his journey. In Buenos Aires he had already read with interest Vaca Guzmán's book on the Chaco Indians, and he "had marked a page, as though he had the secret feeling that he would succumb to their blows."[4]

The French mission did not make it far downriver. The Indians we are going to meet in this story lived, for the most part, between the San Francisco mission upstream and Cabayurepoti, downstream, though a few groups farther downstream were also implicated. Broadly speaking, Crevaux was preparing to penetrate a region populated by many different Indigenous groups, but which was at the same time curiously homogeneous. With the exception of the Chiriguano people to the west, all of the Indians along the Pilcomayo, while belonging to different language families (Guaykurú, Mataco-Mataguayo, and Tupí-Guarani), had a number of cultural features in common and formed an inextricable, multiethnic network along the river. If today the Bolivian reaches of the Pilcomayo are home to only two ethnic groups (the Weenhayeks and, many fewer in number, the Guarani-speaking Tapietes), in 1882 the landscape was much more varied. At the same time—and this is important—this ethnic landscape differed from the "classic" Chaco precisely because of the presence (more pronounced in the second half of the nineteenth century) of Chiriguano groups.

The Chiriguano people, who are today's Guaranis, did not inhabit the Chaco proper but the Andean foothills, on the western edge of the Chaco. In colonial times, the entire region was known as the Chiriguano cordillera, or "frontier." The Chiriguanos formed a large Indigenous group, which, throughout the entire colonial period and a good part of the nineteenth century, had a reputation as intractable Indians, bloodthirsty barbarians, and the plague of any conquistador, missionary, or settler who ventured into their territory. Yet in the 1850s, in other words under the Republic, Chiriguano resolve began to fray. Despite some violent episodes of armed resistance and a deadly war in 1874–1877, at the beginning of the 1880s Chiriguano people were living for the most part at the Franciscan missions in the foothills or working as day laborers on the lands owned by the "frontier" Criollos. By the 1880s, these once-feared Indians are described as peaceful workers.

Resistance against the *karai* ("whitemen") had not ceased altogether (several bloody uprisings marked the second half of the century), but its

tenor had changed. The range of Indians cooperating to fight colonization had expanded. The first expeditions to the Pilcomayo, in the 1840s,
the development of settlements like Yacuiba or Itiyuru, and the expansion of the Franciscan missions all posed a direct threat to the Indians
of the Chaco, who had formerly been shielded by the Chiriguanos. And
so in the second half of the century, the initiative of resistance passed
to the Chaco, and the few Chiriguanos who continued to fight the advance of the *karai* did so together with the Tobas, Noctenes, and others,
either forgetting or setting aside the former enmity that had opposed
them.

Simultaneously, the number of ethnic "defectors" was on the rise, as in
the case of those Chiriguanos who left for the plains of the Chaco, which
were still free, and settled among the groups on the Pilcomayo. This was
the case of the brothers Cototo and Socó, whom we will meet on several
occasions, whose father was a Chiriguano man from the Tarairi mission
and whose mother was Toba. We find them sometimes in Tarairi and
sometimes with the Tobas, but they are always hostile to missionaries
and other explorers. Similarly, Apiguaiqui, the messianic leader of the
last Chiriguano uprising in 1892 in Kuruyuki, carried a Toba name, and
we should probably identify him as another of those "defectors" whose
numbers were on the rise in those years.

These alliances, these comings and goings, shaped the ethnic landscape of the region and stamped the upper Pilcomayo with its own
character, in opposition to the panorama prevailing downstream where
Chiriguano influence was less apparent. For a time, the wars between
Chiriguanos and Chaco Indians in this region gave way to Indigenous
alliances against the settlers.

Primus inter pares among the Chaco Indians fighting alongside the
Chiriguanos and now directing the resistance to colonization were the
Tobas. Like most Guaykurú-speaking groups of the Chaco, the Tobas
had adopted the horse early on, which made them particularly formida-
ble enemies. In 1882 they were living on the left bank of the Pilcomayo,
downstream from the San Francisco mission. The narrow band of
Choroti territory separated them from the Tobas downstream, known
in Argentina as "Western Tobas" or "Toba-Pilagas"; farther downstream
still were the Pilagas, who were closely allied with the Tobas. The Pilagas
are sometimes called Orejones or Orejudos in old sources, referring to
their earlobes artificially lengthened by their ornaments.

Relations seem to have been unstable between the various groups
along the Pilcomayo. At times they appear to be allies, as at Fort Bella

Esperanza in 1866, when the upstream Tobas stole some horses and called those downstream to their aid;[5] at other times, on the contrary, a state of war prevailed.

In 1859, as a prelude to their (relative) acceptance of the Christian mission, a fraction of the upstream Tobas signed a peace treaty with the frontier Criollos, under the auspices of the Franciscan brothers.[6] The following year, they opted for the Catholic mission as protection from the settlers' advance, and thus the San Francisco Solano mission on the Pilcomayo was born. But we should not be misled by this acceptance after decades of bitter fighting. The Tobas used the mission as a refuge, always temporary, for their families, their women and children, their old people, or their sick; in 1878 the missionary at San Francisco complained, "There are days when the only residents at the mission are adolescents, the old, and the sick."[7] It is true that the main Toba actors in our story, like young Yallá or the leaders Peloco, Caligagae, etc., appear as often in the mission and under the protection the Franciscans as in their own camps downstream.

The mission is thus the theater of constantly shifting relations, problems, flight, and attacks by neophytes or their downstream kin. Such was the case in 1873, when on September 27, one hundred Tobas from the mission fled downstream to Teyu at the command of a certain Cuserai or Cusarai, "a presumptuous, insolent young man." The missionary relating this episode suggests that Cuserai was driven to flight and "insolence" by the Criollos of the neighborhood, who "either from need of or from greed for labor wanted our Tobas to get used to [living] there where they would be easier to exploit."[8] These sporadic flights and assaults were the prelude to the bloody war of 1874 that ravaged the whole frontier until 1877, which was the high point of the fighting alliances between Tobas and Chiriguanos.

The Indigenous uprising was put down harshly. After their defeat, many of the Chiriguano rebels fled to the banks of the Pilcomayo and into Toba territory. The Franciscans took several Chiriguano families to the San Francisco mission in the hope of restoring peace and holding up an example of obedience. A few years later, four Toba "captains"[9]— Cuserai, Yñiri, Chacari, and Calicagai—petitioned for reincorporation in the mission; this was granted subject to conditions and with the exception of the "caudillo Cuserai."[10]

But even though they were the principal actors, the Chiriguanos and the Tobas were not alone in the 1874 uprising: groups of Noctenes and Tapietes also took part. The Noctenes, or Notenes, are the present-day

Weenhayeks of Bolivia, known as Wichís in Argentina. In 1863 some of them joined the ephemeral Bella Esperanza mission, which was later moved to San Antonio de Padua, across from the San Francisco mission. Farther downriver and still on the right bank we find the Mataguayos and, at Piquirenda, the Güisnays, whose leader in the 1880s was Sirome or Silomi.

"Famous" and "renowned," Sirome's prestige was "recognized by numerous tribes to the south and north of his usual residence."[11] In September 1881, Sirome had accepted the invitation of several settlers from Yacuiba (among whom was a certain Martín Barroso) to found a settlement at Piquirenda and was in discussion with the Franciscans to establish a mission on their land.

Although less present in our story, other groups complete the ethnic kaleidoscope of this stretch of the Pilcomayo. Downstream from Cabayurepoti were the Chorotes or Chorotis. Farther downstream, below Piquirenda on the left bank, at the Patiño Falls, were the Indians today known as Nivaclés and at the time Tapietes—not to be confused with the "other" Tapietes, a Guarani-language group also living in the Chaco region, but in the interior.

If the simple enumeration of the ethnic groups living in the region at the time that interests us can be confusing or exhausting, this impression is even greater if we look at relations among the different groups. A list like the above, necessarily organized in a certain way, could suggest well-defined, closed groups living on clearly delineated territories. The contrary is true. The main demarcation criterion for ethnic groups takes into account not so much the riverbank occupied by the group but rather the notions of downstream and upstream.[12] For instance, the downstream Tobas are distinct from the upstream group. That is why the toponyms we will encounter in this story, like Teyu or Cabayurepoti, are not confined to one bank of the Pilcomayo: while it is true that the Tobas lived for the most part on the right bank, and Teyus or Cabayurepoti "proper" had camps on the same side, in reality these names applied to the lands on both sides of the river.

Yesterday as today, the ethnic groups of the Pilcomayo were inextricably bound together by a chain of exchanges, marriage alliances, barter, and war. Merely following the late nineteenth-century explorers is enough to convince one. Toba, Choroti, and Tapiete families were living at Taringuiti (Bella Esperanza) in 1887; farther down the river, at Yanduñanca, Tobas and Noctenes were living together, but also Tapietes and Chorotes, and a little later even some Chiriguanos who had fled

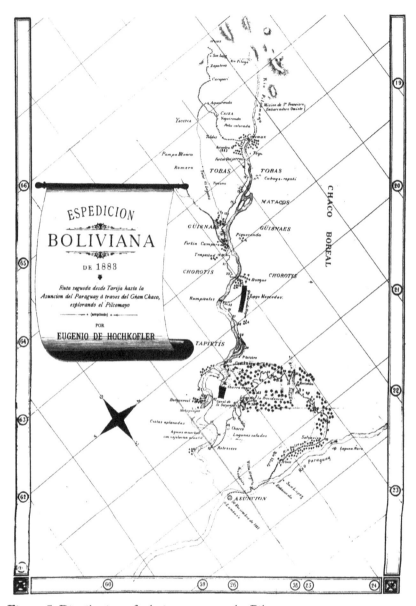

Figure 5. Distribution of ethnic groups on the Pilcomayo
Daniel Campos, De Taríja a la Ascunción (1988).

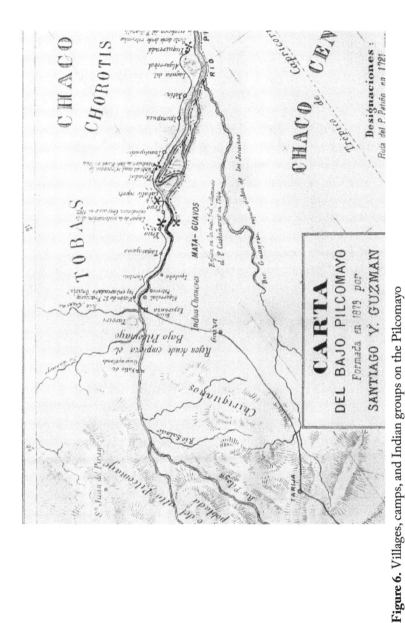

Figure 6. Villages, camps, and Indian groups on the Pilcomayo
Detail of map by Vaca Guzmán, *El Esplorador J. Crevaux* (1882). The map was made in 1879. In 1882, the author added Crevaux's route in red and marked the presumed site of his death with a cross. The "Yuquirenda" on the map is actually "Piquirenda."

to the Chaco after their defeat at Kuruyuki in 1892; the Toba village of Yuarenda, between Teyo and Cabayurepoti, was home to Tobas and some recently established Chorotes. Cabayurepoti was "one of the most remarkable places in the Chaco, which served as a rallying point for barbarian tribes presenting a common interest in serious cases"; it was "the headquarters where a large portion of the northern Chaco tribes gathered to discuss questions of common defense, peace, or war";[13] and around the Crevaux Settlement just upriver, founded on the former site of the Indigenous Teyus, lived Tobas, Tapietes, and Noctenes, but also Chiriguano survivors of the Battle of Kuruyuki.

Toponyms such as *Teyu* (lizard), *Cabayurepoti* (horse manure), *Yanduñanca* (rhea head), or *Piquirenda* (place where there are "sardines," or little fish) come from the Guarani language, which does not mean that a same place cannot have other names in other languages—for instance the Chiriguano *Taringuiti* (place of the cactus) is the Toba *Lagarikallañi* or *Lagarikagattañi*, referring to the same cactus. But in fact, the Guarani spoken by the Chiriguanos seems to have been the lingua franca used along this stretch of the Pilcomayo, at least at this time. For instance, we find Tobas whose name includes the Guarani adjective *guasu*, "big," just as the name Cuserai may contain the Guarani suffix –*rai* ("little"). Similarly, we meet José Correa, a captive of the Tobas for so long that he had forgotten his Spanish mother tongue and testified in Guarani. In a way, the Guarani language was understood by everyone and functioned as a sort of mortar, helping consolidate the pluriethnic mosaic in the Pilcomayo.

This multiethnic fabric is reflected in the makeup of the Indigenous armies that attacked Criollos and travelers. But military alliances were not restricted to the Tobas and the Chiriguanos. Amadeo Baldrich, for example, mentions Tobas, Matacos, "Orejudos" (Pilagas), and "even Chiriguanos" banding together to fight Argentinian explorers.[14] Yet even though they were perfectly aware of this situation, the Criollos accused, time and again, always, and only, the Tobas. Having inherited the Chiriguanos' role of villains, the Tobas had the worst reputation and were blamed for everything bad that happened. Every theft together with the lamentable situation of the settlers on the frontier was attributed to these "desert Bedouins." On March 6, 1882, just before Jules Crevaux left for the Pilcomayo, General Jofré warned him:

> The Tobas and the Matacos are those that occupy the better part
> of the banks of the Pilcomayo; and as they are the cleverest and

Figure 7. "Toba and Choroti Indians at Ivibobo, left bank of the Pilcomayo, Gran Chaco" (1903)
Photo by Jean-Baptiste Vaudry, in Isabelle Combès and Michèle Salaun, eds., *El Chaco de Jean-Baptiste Vaudry* (2018), p. 103.

strongest of the Gran Chaco tribes, they dominate all the others. A secret instinct seems to warn them that their wandering life and absolute empire over these vast territories will end when outright and reliable communication is established between the republics of Paraguay and Bolivia. Obstinately resistant to civilization, their system consists in the destruction of everything that does not come from their race. They drag the other tribes into joining them in this degrading occupation and make heroic virtues of plunder and betrayal. As soon as you arrive at the Aguarenda [Aguairenda] mission, emissaries will sneak off to announce to all the tribes the presence of suspicious *carayes* [*karai*], which is what they call white foreigners. From that moment on, you and your companions will be harassed by these savages ... beware of the submissions and alliances or truces they will often propose only to turn around and betray you with or without the slightest pretext.[15]

The Tobas' reputation contrasts with that of their neighbors whom they "bring along" with them. In the eyes of the frontier Criollos of the Chaco, who merely adopt a Chiriguano scale of values, the Tobas are opposed, on the one hand, to the Matacos or the "dirty, degenerate" Noctenes, portrayed as quasi animals in the accounts and, on the other hand, to the Chiriguanos, a more civilized, "superior race" made up of "likeable hard-working natives," who represent "the highest intellectual level among the territories' tribes" and can be regarded as *civilized Indians.*"[16]

These considerations will be important when it comes time to weigh the accusations against the Indians and their degree of guilt in the massacre of the Crevaux expedition. Even if the Tobas were the first and principal suspects from the outset, absolutely all of the groups in the region were accused at one time or another of complicity or of having actually participated in killing the explorers in 1882.

The constant rustling of cattle or the sporadic and problematic presence of Tobas and Noctenes in the Franciscan missions shows this: even if, unlike the Chiriguanos, the Pilcomayo Indians did not live on the settlement frontier, they were far from isolated or inward looking; rather they maintained fluid relations with the Criollos in the borderlands. To the thefts and the missions must be added, in this second half of the nineteenth century and increasingly from the 1870s on, the massive seasonal migrations to the sugar factories in northwest Argentina, such as La Esperanza or Ledesma. Even if these migrations were on the whole temporary, they fostered a greater acquaintance with the colonizing society, the rules of the markets, or new goods. Sirome, the Güisnay leader on the Pilcomayo, often went to Yacuiba or Itiyuru. The difference between the Chiriguanos' situation and that of the Chaco Indians was that the latter *traveled* to the villages, the factories, the missions, or the Criollo estancias; they did not have to put up with the presence of *karai* on their own lands. The initiative was theirs, so to speak. Even in the midst of an international dispute among three countries, the Pilcomayo was still an Indian territory, wholly Indian. That is why the Chiriguanos who still believed in armed struggle took refuge with the Tobas, and that is why *karai* attempts to penetrate the forests of the Chaco were met with violence.

The "whites" of the frontier complete the long list of suspects in the Crevaux case. In the Chaco as elsewhere, the settlement front was represented by a series of actors who were not always on the best of terms. There were, to start, the Franciscan friars from Tarija College, for the most part Italians; Bolivian settlers, big or small cattle ranchers living on their farms and/or in frontier villages; local authorities like the corregidors, subprefects, etc., who were on the whole also settlers and hacienda owners with cattle; and soldiers from the forts or the military settlements.

The truth is, even if in 1882 several forts had been established in Chiriguano territory, and Caiza was theoretically a "military settlement," there was still only one fort on the actual banks of the Pilcomayo, below the San Francisco mission. This was Bella Esperanza, founded by the Rivas/Gianelli expedition in 1863. At the time of the Crevaux expedition, the fort was clearly in decline and the target of sporadic thefts and attacks on the part of the Tobas and other Pilcomayo groups. In 1880, the Bolivian government decreed the construction of a new fort at Ñuapúa and the restoration of Fort Bella Esperanza, entrusting the work to the Criollos of Azero Province (Department of Chuquisaca). But work did not begin until two years later, after the massacre of the Crevaux mission. From that time on, the number of forts and military settlements grew, beginning with the Crevaux Settlement, founded in 1883 by Daniel Campos.

The Franciscan college in Tarija played a large role in founding Fort Bella Esperanza, alongside which Fr. Gianelli built the first Noctene mission: indeed, the government saw the religious missions as favoring the advance of colonization. Already in 1830, the Bolivian government had issued a decree making missions the most effective means to "reduce and to evangelize the remaining unsubjugated Indians." This decree also set in place concrete means of aiding the missions, particularly by endowing them with lands and securing them government economic support. From 1840 on, the missions became one of the main instruments for colonizing Indian territories.

Between 1845 and 1872, Tarija College founded seven missions among the Chiriguanos and two (San Francisco Solano and San Antonio de Padua) on the Pilcomayo, among the Tobas and the Noctenes. In 1882 the county commissioner for the Tarija missions was Fr. Doroteo Giannecchini, one of the principal actors in our story, both detective and suspect in the Crevaux murder and author of some of the most important accounts at our disposal. The Italian friar, originally from Tuscany, was forty-five years old in 1882, with over twenty years of experience in the Chaco frontier missions. He had served as missionary to the Tobas at San Francisco Solano, as parish priest for the Criollos of Caiza, and in the Tarairi, Chimeo, and Aguairenda missions, among the Chiriguanos.

Figure 8. Doroteo Giannecchini
Drawing by Riou in Arthur Thouar, *Explorations dans l'Amérique du Sud* (1891),
p. 39.

Giannecchini was the county commissioner responsible for the Tarija missions from 1877 to 1885. Fluent in the Guarani language spoken by the Chiriguanos and possessing rudiments of the Toba language, he wrote a Chiriguano dictionary and several texts on the history of the missions and the ethnography of their pupils. In a word, he was the most emblematic figure of Tarija College and the most knowledgeable about the Indians of the region. In this capacity, he was a member of the "Promoting Commission" created to mount a new Bolivian expedition to the Pilcomayo and as such became Crevaux's mentor. The explorer himself states: "The Reverend Franciscan Fathers of Tarija convent, who are Italian, provided us with the most valuable information concerning Gran Chaco Indigenous peoples and offered their collaboration in building our boats."[17]

But the missions were not the only presence on the frontier. With or against them were the Bolivian settlers, isolated hacienda owners, and/or people from the bordering populations. The main Criollo centers of the region in 1882 were Caiza (Villa Rodrigo), founded in 1843; Yacuiba, to the south, which grew in importance in the 1870s and later became the

Figure 9. San Francisco Solano Mission (c. 1903)
Photo by Jean-Baptiste Vaudry, in Combès and Salaun, *El Chaco de Jean-Baptiste Vaudry* (2018), p. 93.

administrative capital of the Bolivian Chaco; and Itiyuru, at the time a Bolivian territory but today part of Argentina.

Settlers and missionaries were all in the front ranks of the settlement movement, but their relations were somewhat strained. Initially the missionaries' installation had helped the settlers by pacifying certain parts of the territory, and in fact many haciendas first established themselves under the protection of the Franciscan missions. But later, and especially after the 1874–1877 defeat of the Indians, the missions were no longer as useful to the settlers, who believed they had definitively subjugated the Chiriguanos. Furthermore, access to Indigenous lands and labor soon brought Criollos and missionaries into open opposition: "There was a fatal collision of interests between the missionary Fathers and the landowners in these villages. Everyone was fighting over labor."[18]

In 1871 Father Alejandro Ercole, from Tarija College, drew up the text known as "Mission Regulations," which was adopted by the Bolivian government and, given its origin, was highly favorable to the friars. According to these regulations, the missions were under the direct authority of the national government and did not answer to the local authorities of each region; the neophyte Indians were under their responsibility, and the missions themselves were exempt from taxes. In the event of a new foundation, the lands were to be directly awarded by the executive branch. In exchange the friars were required to provide neophytes as guides and labor for explorations, and to facilitate such expeditions by all means available: this they had already done (Gianelli in 1863) and would continue to do in the following years, collaborating with the Crevaux and Campos expeditions in 1882 and 1883, and participating directly in those led by Rivas (1882) and Thouar (1887).

The privileges awarded the friars aggravated tensions between landowners and the missions. On the Chaco frontier, most settlers were hostile to the new regulations, which deprived them in particular of Indian labor or at least obliged them to pay better than they had been doing. Local authorities also protested, since corregidors—or magistrates— and subprefects were also, or primarily, settlers; in 1882 for instance, the subprefect of Gran Chaco was Eudogio Raña, who participated in the Criollos' expeditions against the Indigenous peoples of the Pilcomayo. Before representing the remote central government and adhering to the law obliging them to help the missionaries, these authorities first looked after their own interests, often contrary to those of the Franciscans.

The settlers thus accused the Franciscans of wanting to monopolize the Indians and of separating them from the national society, and in so doing working against colonization. The influence enjoyed by the friars downriver on the Pilcomayo, stemming from the shuttling back and forth of their Toba and Noctene neophytes, exasperated the ranchers. When the Indians rustled cattle, it was the Franciscans who mediated to recover the animals and, according to Thouar, much to the advantage of the missionaries at the time he was writing; the settlers were made to pay for this service.

> What exasperated the Bolivians in the area about the missionaries was that, in order to recover possession of their animals, they had to pay fifty percent of their value as *rescate* (redemption). This tax, without which the affected owner could not obtain the Fathers' intervention with the Tobas or other Indians for restitution of the stolen animals, made the missions many enemies.[19]

The Franciscans, for their part, protested, and defended themselves by going on the attack. Fr. Corrado insinuated that the flight of the Tobas led by Cuserai in 1870 was actually orchestrated by Criollo neighbors.

Figure 10. A street in Caiza (c. 1903)
Photo by Jean-Baptiste Vaudry, in Combès and Salaun, *El Chaco de Jean-Baptiste Vaudry* (2018), p. 82.

During the same period, presenting himself as a Defender of the Indians and casting veiled accusations at the settlers, Giannecchini also reported: "All of the thefts going on in the Chaco weren't always the Tobas' work. Others, too, were known to steal, because the best animals in the herd often vanished while the others weren't taken. When the Tobas steal, they don't choose, they take everything they find."[20]

The same Giannecchini described the settlers as "Godless, conscienceless adventurers." The missionaries felt that the whites' cruel exploitation of the Indians was the true reason for the uprisings. The history of the colonization of the Chaco was "an Iliad of sins, crimes, and scandals, revenge, cruelty, outrages, thefts, arrogance, and the law of might makes right."[21]

Rivalries, hatreds, and accusations were carried far. At the beginning of 1884, Tarija College reported two attempts to murder the resident priest at Caiza.[22] Already in 1867, during the Sebastián expedition to the Chaco, the mission Fathers were accused of sabotage. Because they were preparing their fields, the mission neophytes refused to accompany the explorers, and the latter accused the Franciscans of trying to sabotage the expedition "because they thought that its results would weaken their

Figure 11. Dr. Crevaux's departure
Drawing by Riou in Thouar, "A la recherche des restes de la mission Crevaux"
(1884), p. 230.

monopoly on the Indians. As they left Caiza, the haughty expedition troops cursed the priests as enemies of progress, and threats to return were heard."[23]

The very same accusations surfaced at the time of the massacre of the Crevaux mission and, later, the failures of the Rivas and Thouar missions. In all three cases, the direct target of the accusations was Doroteo Giannecchini, Crevaux's mentor and chaplain of the disastrous surviving expeditions.

CHAPTER 2

Chronicle of an Announced Death

Jules Crevaux arrived in Tarija on March 4, 1882, followed four days later by Doroteo Giannecchini, who answered the call of the "Promoting Commission" responsible for organizing a new expedition to the Pilcomayo. With the arrival of the European explorers, the Bolivian government offered to combine the two expeditions and proposed its direction to the young Frenchman. But Crevaux refused: he preferred to set off immediately with a smaller group of companions while the Pilcomayo was in full spate. Giannecchini's primary task was therefore to aid the young explorer who, furthermore, had arrived in Tarija with recommendations from high Franciscan authorities in Argentina.

One of Giannecchini's main concerns was to try to facilitate and ensure, to the best of his ability, the relations the French explorer needed to forge with the Pilcomayo Indians. Like everyone, the Franciscan knew that several of these Indians lived in Tarija, as household help and war booty. He therefore took a first important measure to protect the man he considered "his close friend": he would free one of these captives, a Toba girl, daughter of an important headman, and send her to her people as a peace ambassadress. Everyone thought this was an excellent idea, with the exception of the girl's respectable "owner," who demanded financial compensation for the loss of his servant. The prefecture paid him and added other gifts for Yallá, the young Toba girl, known in Spanish as Petrona. She was fourteen and had been captured a year earlier by Martín Barroso, a Criollo from Yacuiba—this was the same Barroso

Figure 12. Crevaux's farewells
Crevaux's calling card, verso, private archives of Virginio Lema, Tarija. Text, translated: "Rendez-vous on a Paris sidewalk after exploring the Pilcomayo, to my friend the Marquis of Campero. Tarija, 14 mars 1882. Jules Crevaux."

who, at the time, was negotiating with Sirome to establish a settlement in Piquirenda among the Güisnay.

On March 13, Crevaux set out for the Pilcomayo, and, the following day, Giannecchini and Yallá joined him at Ivitivi before reaching the Chaco. The explorer grew fond of the Indian girl. He was going to need her even more than he thought: in effect, at Ivitivi, the bad news came: the Caiza settlers had left two days earlier on an expedition to punish some Pilcomayo Indians for having stolen horses. We know the name of several of these settlers: David Gareca, a certain Lea-Plaza, Gerónimo Miranda, and Eudogio Raña.1 Giannecchini was frightened, fearing that the Tobas' revenge would fall on the Crevaux mission that was about to leave.

The Franciscan, but also Crevaux and Martín Barroso, wrote immediately to the subprefect of Gran Chaco in protest, requesting that the expedition from Caiza be called off. But in vain, and for a very good reason: the subprefect was none other than Eudogio Raña, a member of the Criollo expedition. On March 30, "the sinister expedition" was back, with seven Noctene captives. Five of them, children, were turned over to the San Francisco mission; the others had been wounded and were kept in Caiza.

Given these circumstances, Yallá became their only hope, though a faint one, to ensure the success of the Crevaux mission. On April 4, she left the San Francisco mission for her parents' house downriver. Giannecchini showered her with recommendations and messages for the "Toba, Choroti, and Noctene captains"—the Franciscan was

Figure 13. Yallá, also known as Petrona
Drawing by Théophile Novis (Archives Nationales, F/17/3009B, dossier Thouar).

altogether familiar with the ethnic mosaic of the Pilcomayo. The girl also carried special recommendations for her father, the Toba headman, Caligagae.

Meanwhile Crevaux was busy having his boats made by neophytes at the Tarairi and San Francisco missions. Several authors write of a total of three boats; Crevaux indicates that there were four, all with flat bottoms. The explorer also continued to gather information on the Indians he would meet along the way; he consulted the Chiriguano grammar compiled by the Franciscans and, with Giannecchini's help, he made a phrase book of Toba and Mataco terms.

The boats were ready, but Yallá did not return. Crevaux decided to set off anyway, even though the situation was rather worrisome. On April 8, there had been a first outbreak of violence when a group of Tobas killed two Chiriguanos from the Machareti mission and captured their wives. The Franciscans unhesitatingly ascribed this incident to a Toba revenge: "Here you have the first effect of the Criollos' expedition!"[2] For their part, the inhabitants of Caiza offered to accompany Crevaux as far as Teyu; but when the time came, the explorer left without them. In the Criollos' version, Crevaux himself refused their help: "he didn't accept anything," "he did not want to accept … he refused everything."[3] Their departure was set for April 19, and the boats launched from what was known as the "Omiste" ramp, so called in honor of the Bolivian diplomat at the San Francisco Solano mission. Two days earlier, Crevaux had written to the Minister of Finance and Industry, Antonio Quijarro:

> There are seventeen of us, five French, two Argentinian naval officers, eight young Bolivians, a child of fifteen, Bolivian as well, and a Chiriguano Indian who will act as our interpreter. We have four boats that we had built here. They are very simple craft, but flat bottomed, which draw barely ten or fifteen centimeters when loaded. Two of them are so light, made of cedar, that, if need be, they can be carried on a man's back. We are taking *charque* [jerky], three live sheep, ten chickens, and bags of pulses like beans, corn, rice, biscuits, two small barrels of eau-de-vie, for forty-five days of travel … The prefect of Tarija sent me a large quantity of trinkets to exchange with the Indians we meet. I harbor the hope that my mission will succeed, but I foresee serious difficulties that will need to be overcome. Obviously the Indians, who are agitated over a recent expedition from Caiza that killed some Matacos, will receive us badly. These savages will not want to believe in the good faith of our words of peace.[4]

The time for goodbyes came: "All of us were moved, the French, the crew members, the Christians, and the Indians, as though we had an instinctive foreboding."[5] Naturally later publications, which already knew how the story ended, were full of such premonitions. As Crevaux had made his confession before setting out, "his companions were troubled, panic-stricken because they all understood the danger they were risking."[6] The French helmsman was reported also to have asked to make his confession before leaving, with these hard words: "I have a terrible feeling, we are going to die at the hands of the Tobas … I would like to see Crevaux die on the spot, because his death would be our salvation, this man is leading us directly to slaughter."[7]

Crevaux had thought it would take a month to reach Asunción: the journey lasted only nine days. Beginning to follow his route downriver meant negotiating a slippery, uncertain terrain. We know the details thanks to three testimonies: that of the Chiriguano Indian, Yahuanahua, who alerted the local authorities in Caizu and Itiyuru to the massacre and was questioned by the subprefect, Raña; a letter written by an anonymous Franciscan from the San Francisco mission, dated June 1882—the letter was transcribed and published by Santiago Vaca Guzmán, and

Figure 14. Massacre of the Crevaux mission
Drawing by Riou in Thouar, *Explorations dans l'Amérique du Sud* (1891), p. 43.

forms the basis of an newspaper article by Luis Paz; finally, we have the crucial testimony of Francisco Zeballos, a young Criollo from Yacuiba and a surviving member of the expedition. Zeballos was questioned by Giannecchini, Marcelleti, and by the correspondents of several Tarija newspapers in July 1882.

On April 19 in the afternoon, the travelers came to Irua, where Crevaux writes to Giannecchini: "We have made peace with the Tobas. I am sending them to you. We have gone eight leagues without incident."8 The Noctenes from the village carried this message to the San Francisco mission, where it aroused a certain perplexity after the massacre. The Franciscan author of the letter dated June 8 exclaims: "The poor man!! He did not know these were not Toba Indians and that they were harmless, and he thought he already had the enemies of civilization at his feet."9

When they reached Irua, Crevaux took on a Noctene Indian named Calisin to guide them as far as Teyu. On April 20, the boats passed within view of Bella Esperanza. According to the young Zeballos, the Indians had seemed slightly hostile during the night, but a rifle shot chased them off. The first information gathered before Zeballos was rescued indicated the contrary: "From Bella Esperanza, a crowd of savages on foot and on horseback followed the boats that were gliding down the river without incident. Satisfied to see that crowds were drawn by the gifts they were beginning to distribute, the crew had no fears and, on the contrary, lost all wariness."[10]

April 21 and 22 passed without incident, and the explorers arrived at Teyu on the afternoon of the 22nd. According to the letter dated June 8, there they met the Toba Indian, Cuserai, whom we already know, surrounded by a large number of Indians whom Vaca Guzmán identifies as Tobas and Chiriguanos. The Indians gave them a warm welcome and promised to guide them as far as Cabayurepoti. In Teyu, Crevaux slept in the Indian camp, and even had the guns emptied of ammunition to avoid any risk of an incident. It was at Teyu that, according to the San Francisco missionary, the Tobas deliberated whether or not to kill the explorers—opinion was apparently divided. Whatever the case, Luis Paz writes, "Barbary prevailed among the barbarians." The Noctene guide from Irua tried to warn Crevaux of the danger but without success: the Frenchman did not believe there was any. Calisin fled.

As Francisco Zeballos tells it, on April 23 and 24 the travelers passed through Cabayurepoti without incident. All was calm on the 25th, the boats continued their journey and negotiated a falls a short way downriver from Cabayurepoti. April 27 finally came. The members of the expedition, or at least the majority, went ashore, and the Indians attacked them, killing (almost) everyone. According to Giannecchini (who does not miss a chance to blame the Caiza Criollos), the crime took place in the vicinity of the villages attacked a month earlier by the settlers' expedition. Yet in Yahuanahua's version, repeated by the Criollos, rather than an act of revenge, the immediate cause of the massacre was the gifts handed out right and left by Crevaux: the Indians killed the travelers in order to appropriate the goods of the expedition.[11] In Caiza, Eudogio Raña learned what had happened on May 2, in the evening. Either because they suspected something, or they felt guilty for not having accompanied the explorers as they had promised, the people of Caiza and the military commander, Fernando Soruco, set a Chiriguano Indian, Yahuanahua, on Crevaux's trail. Arriving in Teyu, Yahuanahua saw the remains of a boat floating on the river, and some Indians told him what had happened.

Upon his return, Yahuanahua gave the news first of all to Baltazar Guerrero, commander of Itiyuru, who immediately alerted Raña. As so often in such cases, Yahuanahua was immediately suspected of complicity and "he was presumed to have been the spy who warned the Tobas of the explorers' upcoming trip."[12]

On May 11, the massacre hit the front pages of the Tarija newspapers, and *El Trabajo* announced: "Special from the Gran Chaco. The Crevaux expedition fails. He and all of his companions murdered by Tobas in their capital, Teyo. The sad news sparked deep emotion in our society when we learned the news from the special courier from Gran Chaco yesterday."[13] Two days later, the Tarija prefect communicated the reports to the Bolivian government, still harboring the thin hope that they might be false. But the contrary was to prove true. At the end of the month, the Buenos Aires newspaper *La Nación* published a telegram sent by Francisco Arraya, subprefect of Tupiza, a Bolivian town on the border with Argentina: "The disastrous death of Dr. Crevaux and his companions in exploring the Pilcomayo has been confirmed."[14]

According to Eudogio Raña, relying on Yahuanahua's report, the killing took place in Teyu; according to a letter from one San Francisco missionary, written June 8, it took place at Cabayurepoti; and in Zeballos's version, it happened downstream from that site. There where Zeballos spoke only of Tobas, Raña stated that the killing had been planned by the Tobas, the Chiriguanos, and the "Tapietis [*sic*]"; the June 8 letter mentions the Tobas and the Chiriguanos but also the presence of "many tribes" at Cabayurepoti. The first reports were already very confused, and there was major uncertainty about what really happened. While the disastrous news was crossing the ocean and the first homages were being organized in Argentina and in France, the first investigations into the crime were also getting under way.

CHAPTER 3

Searching for the Remains of the Crevaux Mission

The death of Crevaux and his companions did not produce an official police investigation—a tacit acknowledgment on the part of the authorities that the Indians on the Pilcomayo lay outside their jurisdiction. The actual detectives were private individuals: Franciscans, geographers and explorers, soldiers sent on punitive expeditions, or local authorities. Each conducted their investigation for their own purposes or on behalf of the French and Argentinian geographical societies; they did not coordinate their efforts, and there was no higher authority responsible for collecting and analyzing the information. Furthermore, a good number of these amateur detectives were also (or initially) suspected of complicity or worse. This was the case for the Franciscans in general and of Doroteo Giannecchini in particular, or of Eudogio Raña, the Gran Chaco sub-prefect and member of the expedition organized by the Caiza settlers in March 1882.

As for the states involved (Bolivia, Argentina, and France), the initiatives taken were aimed more at punishment than at any real criminal investigation, and even though the expeditions were described as "rescue missions," they were too long in getting organized. In the no-man's-land that is the Pilcomayo for all practical purposes, any detective runs the risk of ending up like the victims. Which means that, in the following months, investigators learned only what the Indians were disposed to tell them, and recovered only the objects the same Indians were willing to turn over. Not much more. Here we need to take a close look at

Figure 15. Death of Dr. Crevaux
Jules Gros, "Mort du Dr Crevaux" (1882), p. 300.

the initial investigations, at the material evidence discovered, and at the interrogations to which witnesses and suspects were subjected. Even if these yielded more doubts than certainties, they are the only material in our possession with which to at least partially reconstruct the story behind Crevaux's death. The first investigations began in May 1882, immediately after the massacre was announced, with Arthur Thouar's expedition to the Chaco.

Although in May 1882, Eudogio Raña announced his intention to go to Teyu to rescue possible survivors and/or to punish the culprits, and to that end asked for fifty neophytes as backup, there is no indication that he really left. On the contrary, the settlers sent a delegation of Indians ("subjugated Matacos") to find out what was going on; they returned a few days later, for fear of the Tobas, without having learned anything.

The first expedition to set out in search of the remains of the Crevaux expedition left at the end of July (three months after the crime); this was an Argentinian initiative entrusted to Luis Jorge Fontana, a veteran of the Pilcomayo explorations. Inexplicably, the Fontana mission decided to navigate up the river from its entrance to the Paraguay River, instead of descending its course as Crevaux had done. Which suggests that this expedition was also undertaken on a whim of the Argentinian government. Whatever the truth may be, Fontana was forced to turn back at the end of August because the river was too low for navigation and because he had mistakenly embarked on a "false branch" of the Pilcomayo, which later became known as the "Fontana branch." As for Crevaux and his unfortunate companions, the expedition discovered strictly nothing.

It was the Bolivian side that came up with more new information in the days and months following the crime. In mid-June, two Toba Indians appeared at the San Francisco mission, sent by their leader Pelocolijiguaso. Pelocolijiguaso is someone we will meet again, under the names of Pelocolic or, as here, Pelocoliqui-guasu, "Big Pelocoliqui," with the addition of a Guarani adjective. The Tobas offered to Fr. Vicente Marcelleti to turn over Francisco Zeballos and a Chiriguano from Tigüipa mission, the interpreter for the Crevaux mission, who survived the massacre and were taken prisoner.[1]

Estanislao Zeballos, a master carpenter from Yacuiba, had effectively been one of the expedition members as well as one of the victims. His son, Francisco, a child of twelve or fifteen, was with him. The Franciscans paid the sum of thirty-six pesos for Francisco's recovery to the fifty Tobas who arrived on July 1 with their captive in a deplorable state.[2]

In the days that followed, Francisco was interviewed by a Tarija newspaper and he told them what he knew. He had managed to escape that day after having seen his companions die, but:

a Toba caught up with him and speared him in the leg; another arrived, tore him away from his aggressor, and took him to Cabayurepoti and from there to Teyu, where the father of Petrona, the Toba girl Crevaux had taken with him from Tarija, and another Toba captain, turned him over to Fr. Vicente Marceleti [sic] at the San Francisco mission as a peace offering and to make up for their abominable murder.[3]

A few days later, at the same mission, Fr. Vicente met with the Toba captains Caligagae (Yallá's father), Iñiri, and Cutaicoliqui. All pleaded their innocence and accused the downriver Tobas; they also implicated the Güisnay and their leader, Sirome or Silomi, saying that he had sent the killers to avenge the death of his father, who had been killed a few years earlier by the settler Cornelio Ríos.[4] In August, in the company of Pelocoliqui-guasu, the same Tobas reasserted their innocence, but no one believed them. The subprefect and the missionaries ordered them to denounce the killers and to return Crevaux's belongings, failing which "it would no longer be a question of peace, but of war, and a war of extermination"—it was Giannecchini, usually a champion of the Indians' cause against the Criollos, who made these threats.[5]

At the same time, the missionaries and the settlers began recovering some of the travelers' effects. At the beginning of May, a Toba showed up at the San Francisco mission wearing the jacket of Jean Dumigron, one of Crevaux's French companions.[6] But the frontier settlers' main concern was the weapons the expedition had been carrying, which were now in the Indians' hands. That was why Eudogio Raña wanted to organize a punitive expedition to the Pilcomayo at the beginning of May to recover the weapons, which the Tobas could use against Caiza. The Indians were "good shots," he said. According to him there were fourteen rifles, three shotguns, and four revolvers.

In Buenos Aires, the Argentinian government had given Crevaux nineteen Remingtons, and his men had three hundred rounds each. Aware of several incidents between Argentinian expeditions and the Indians, Crevaux had expressed his gratitude. Yet these weapons had already disappeared before the French reached Bolivia, in the course of a fairly unclear episode in mid-January of 1882, north of Jujuy, probably at Tumbaya. When they arrived in this village, the explorers are said to have forced a store owner to lodge them, showing him their weapons to intimidate him. The police arrested them during the night and, in the course of the ensuing fight, one of Crevaux's men was wounded in the hand. Crevaux managed to restore calm, but four revolvers, some knives, and a telescope had disappeared, and the police had confiscated the rifles. The travelers spent a night in jail and then were set free after having paid a fine. But they left without their weapons.[7]

Crevaux was therefore obliged to try to obtain new weapons to continue his journey. He asked the Potosi regiment to supply them, and their commanding officer replied that he was willing to send the rifles and ammunition requested. Two days before setting off, Crevaux described his weaponry in the last letters he sent from the San Francisco mission: "Our armory is composed of twelve Remington rifles (infantry model) and fifteen hundred cartridges belonging to the Bolivian government. We also have two other good Lefaucheux rifles and one hundred rounds that can be used for hunting."[8]

In all events, these weapons were now in the hands of the killers, and the people of Caiza were afraid: "The inhabitants [of Caiza] have only six rifles, whereas the savages have all the weapons they took from Dr. Crevaux's expedition."[9] But we notice a contradiction in the settlers' statements: there where Raña feared the Tobas would use the rifles,

Figure 16. Tumbaya, where the Crevaux expedition was arrested
Théophile Novis (Archives Nationales, F/17/3009B, dossier Thouar).

"good shots" as they are, others thought that, if there were still any survivors of the massacre, the Tobas would oblige them to teach them how to use the guns:

> We inhabitants of this vice-canton [*sic*, sous canton] are expecting to be attacked by these enemies from one moment to the next, and we also think that, with the dead men's weapons, they will be able to mount an operation because the captives will teach them how they work.[10] We are exposed in this village, and even more now with the weapons the Tobas have taken, and if they leave one of the expedition members alive, it's even worse because they will make him teach them how to use the rifles.[11]

This seems rather dubious, and Raña's fear has more basis. Even if, at that time, the Tobas usually attacked with their traditional weapons (spears, arrows, or clubs), they had known the settlers for a long time, and this was not the first time they had stolen guns. During the wars that rocked the border in the second half of the century (in 1874–1877 and 1892), we know the Indians knew how to use guns.

Whatever the case may be, the Criollos were unable to recover any of the weapons from the Crevaux expedition in the days and months that followed. Only one revolver surfaced, much later, at the end of 1885 or the beginning of 1886, and was turned in to the Franciscans by some Toba Indians.[12] More than ten years after the crime, allusions to the expedition's guns having fallen into Toba hands could still be found. While on a visit to the region in 1893, Manuel Othon Jofré noted that the Tayasuñanca Tobas had two Remington rifles and ammunition. The Indians claimed they had bought them from the soldiers at the Taringuiti fort, but Jofré thought "that these were instead remains of the Crevaux expedition, because in addition to the rifles, the Indians also had nice cartridge belts, which the guns at the Taringuiti fort did not have."[13]

But even if the weapons were lost, other material evidence appeared over the following months. According to Francisco Zeballos's testimony, the explorers' belongings, some of which had been carefully preserved—for instance, chronometers and watches, worn around the neck—were in Toba hands. Several of these objects were circulating among the various Indian groups on the Pilcomayo and even as far as the border. In September, some coins turned up:

> Although the Tobas had always claimed they knew nothing about Mr. Crevaux and his belongings, they demonstrated the contrary; in effect, the neophytes of the San Francisco mission showed (on September 22) several coins to the friar who had converted them, asking him what sort of medallions these were, because they had holes in them. The Tobas had given them in exchange for supplies. The missionary quickly identified them as coins belonging to the travelers; he recovered them, giving the neophytes twenty centimes a coin.[14]

Thouar, too, reports the incident: "Four twenty-franc coins were turned in by the San Francisco missionaries to the subprefect of Tarija. Some Noctene Indians had come to the mission one day seeking to exchange them for corn and tobacco, and the Chiriguano Indians to whom they had been paid asked the missionary *what were these medallions!*"[15]

Even if this did not constitute proof (people and things travel widely in the Indigenous Chaco, and Crevaux's effects followed the same routes), the incident did not work in favor of the Tobas ... or the Noctenes, in Thouar's version. The San Francisco missionary handed over the coins to Giannecchini, who passed them on to the government delegate, Andrés

Rivas, who was about to set off on a new expedition to the Pilcomayo. Rivas left them with the Aguairenda mission until his return, and, in November 1882, Giannecchini finally sent them to the prefect of Tarija, who signed a receipt. The receipt listed "five napoleons and one pound sterling taken from the Tobas and belonging to Mister Jules Crevaux."[16]

Bernardo Trigo mentions another incident: an Indian woman arrived at the San Francisco mission wearing a black and red necklace with a gold medallion, which a woman in Tarija had given Yallá. Without anyone understanding really why, the medallion was considered to be proof that the Indians who killed Crevaux were the same that, later in November, attacked the Rivas expedition.

Finally, we must mention two episodes that occurred in the same month of September, thanks to which some soldiers recovered yet another relic from the Crevaux mission. In 1880 the Bolivian government had approved the founding of two more military forts on the banks of the Pilcomayo, charging soldiers from Azero Province with their construction. In September, Nicanor Centeno, responsible for restoring the Bella Esperanza fort at Taringuiti, left Tarairi with thirty men. A few hundred meters from the mission, he met the Toba Socó, who was coming to the mission, unarmed. Centeno ordered him to be taken prisoner and shortly afterwards had him executed with fifteen other Tobas, for no reason other than to appropriate the Indians' horses. Following this incident, many Tobas left the San Francisco mission, taking donkeys with them, "and in this way, according to their custom, they declared war."[17] During the same period, on September 4, the soldiers from Azero, who were working on the second fort at Ñuapúa, also had a run-in with a group of Tobas, whom they drove off but not without their taking some satchels, straps, "and a pair of boots belonging to one of the deceased foreigners."[18]

The first evidence gathered on Crevaux's death traveled from the Pilcomayo to the missions and forts along the frontier: from October 1882, however, it was the *karai* who entered or tried to enter the Chaco and who continued to gather information about the killing.

On October 1, the expedition led by Andrés Rivas finally set out. This was the mission the "Promoting Commission" had begun to prepare before Crevaux arrived in Tarija. Doroteo Giannecchini accompanied the soldiers in the roles of chaplain and interpreter. From Caiza the soldiers made for the place called Iguopeiti in Guarani ("the place where the carobs grow") and Santa Bárbara or Santa Bárbara de Teyu by the Criollos, on the right bank of the Pilcomayo; two leagues farther downstream, on

Figure 17. Fort at Ñuapúa
Teófilo Novis, *El Chaco en imágenes* ([1887] 2016), p. 123.

the other bank, was the Toba camp of Teyu. At Santa Bárbara, the Rivas commission was beginning preparations to establish a military settlement. On October 16, a plank measuring a meter and a half was found; it was from one of Crevaux's boats.[19]

The problems began on November 3. Several soldiers set off downstream, along the river, to clear a way to Cabayurepoti. A group of Tobas attacked them and stole no fewer than 250 animals, killing four men. Furious, Rivas declared a "war of extermination" on the Tobas. And the extermination was not long in coming: on November 6, but not exactly as the commander had foreseen. That day, fourteen Tobas arrived at Santa Bárbara, accompanied by a Noctene nicknamed "the Gimp": they wanted to turn over the expedition mules, one of which belonged to Giannecchini and which had become lost upstream somewhere around Yanduñanca. According to Giannecchini's report, Rivas wanted to capture the Indians, but his soldiers got ahead of him and opened fire. A confused fight ensued with the Tobas defending themselves, the soldiers firing left and right, and killing each other, leaving seven *karai* and the fourteen Tobas dead.20

Although Giannecchini's report assigns full responsibility to Rivas's soldiers, who reportedly provoked the Tobas, others did not see it like that. For Paz Guillén, a member of another expedition, it was the Indians who started the fight on that fatal November 6; Baldrich mentions the Rivas expedition, "decimated by thirteen or fourteen Tobas"; and an anonymous letter from Yacuiba does not hesitate to assert that Rivas was surprised by "more than two thousand Tobas!" Taking his cue from Thouar's account, André Bresson later maintains that the Tobas murdered the soldiers "with uncannily refined cruelty."[21] Whatever the case may be, the expedition turned back the following day.

Whether it was because his account decidedly favored the Tobas, or because the Indians claimed they were returning his mule, or, more generally, because of the tensions prevailing between Franciscans and settlers, many blamed Giannecchini directly for the expedition's failure. Yet the settlers had no proof, and no formal complaint was made.

Caiza immediately organized an expedition to punish the Indians and recover the stolen animals. The men left on November 18. At Santa Bárbara, the Tobas had burned the camp and desecrated the graves of the seven killed soldiers. The next day, slightly to the north, the Criollos had managed to recover a few animals and something else: "They found a small, locked box belonging no doubt to Mr. Crevaux; but when they got to Caiza, it was handed around, with no one able to ascertain if it contained a chronometer, a theodolite, a camera, or money."[22]

It is also possible that the box contained a barometer, later turned over, together with the section of plank mentioned by Giannecchini, to the Bolivian authorities. In effect, Daniel Campos later writes: "The superintendant of police [of Tarija], Mr. Ichazo, had recovered a barometer from a fort and a damaged marker belonging to Mr. Crevaux. He turned them over to me together with an official letter and, along with another letter, I gave them to Mr. Thouar."[23] It seems that this was the same instrument that later became a chronometer, which the prefect of Tarija intended to return to the Franciscans in 1884, "in order to help them with the work undertaken in the San Roque temple, for which they were in want of funds."[24]

In 1883 a new Argentinian expedition was organized, which began in June and was led by Rudecindo Ibaceta. It left from Fort Dragones and arrived on the right bank of the Pilcomayo, across from Piquirenda, and then navigated upstream to Teyu and Caiza (where it arrived on August 8), returning to Argentina via Yacuiba. Amadeo Baldrich participated in this expedition, representing the Instituto Geográfico Argentino, and indicated "discovery of the stern of the boat commanded by Crevaux and two or three objects belonging to his martyred companions, relics that we presented to the Institute upon our return, in a public ceremony."[25]

Baldrich adds that "the authenticity of this piece [of the boat] was confirmed in Caiza by a young man named Zeballos, a survivor of this expedition that ended so painfully." But according to Natalio Roldán, the Argentinian mission recovered more than that. Familiar with the northern Chaco, Roldán was not part of the Ibaceta expedition, but he tasked the officers with looking for any object belonging to Crevaux and his men. They recovered the following objects: two jacaranda clubs; a whistle; two spears; two shirts made of *chaguar* (*Bromelia serra*) fiber; a necklace of small white stone beads, two meters long; a bow and two arrows; and three *chaguar* pouches. All of that, which belonged to the Indians and not to members of the Crevaux expedition, was reported to have been found under the planks of Crevaux's boat[26]—though it seems odd that, more than a year after the crime, these objects were still in the same place, awaiting the arrival of the Argentinians.

If Baldrich and Ibaceta encountered Francisco Zeballos in Caiza, it was because the young man was helping prepare a new Bolivian expedition to the Pilcomayo. This was the Campos expedition, which remained famous in the annals because it was the only one that actually reached Asunción. That was not its primary goal, though, which was to establish settlements and forts at Teyu, Cabayurepoti, and Piquirenda. The decision to push on to the Paraguay was taken upon arriving at the Chaco frontier. Although it marked a turning point in the long series of Bolivian expeditions to the Chaco, this one interests us here for other reasons: because it was the one that founded the military settlement at Santa Bárbara de Teyu, baptized Crevaux Settlement in homage to the murdered explorer; and because one of its members was the Frenchman, Arthur Thouar, whose goal was to discover everything he could about the massacre of the Crevaux mission and the possible existence of survivors.

As Thouar himself explains, to the persistent rumors about the existence of survivors was added, in January 1883, a letter written by one Milhomme, a Frenchman living in Carapari, a short distance to the west of Caiza. This letter, together with the rest of Francisco Zeballos's testimony, claimed that two survivors had been captured by the Tobas and that some Chiriguano Indians had seen them. The letter was sent to Ferdinand de Lesseps, president of the Société de Géographie de Paris, who passed it to the Ministry of Foreign Affairs. The Ministry in turn sent it to the French authorities in Santiago de Chile, where Émile Arthur Thouar, a thirty year old with some experience of travel in South

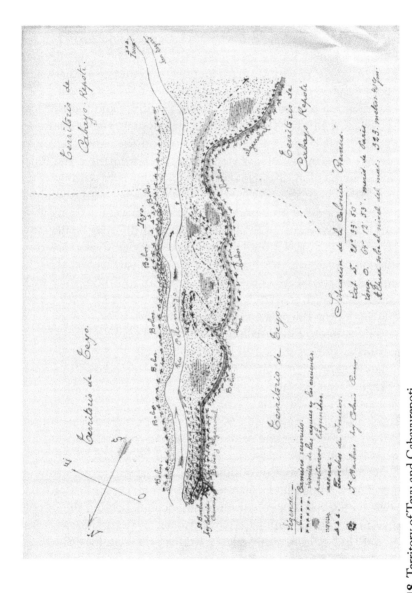

Figure 18. Territory of Teyu and Cabayurepoti
Drawing by Arthur Thouar, August 26, 1883 (Archivo y Biblioteca Nacionales de Bolivia [Sucre] MI 215/32).

America, was to be found. Taking advantage of his presence, the French tasked him with the search for possible survivors.[27]

So Thouar left Santiago and, after having gone through La Paz and Sucre, arrived in Tarija. From there he planned to leave on his own or with a small group for the Pilcomayo. According to the North American journal, *Science*, he even intended to disguise himself and travel as a friar.[28] But his plan was judged extremely dangerous, and it was decided that Thouar should go with Campos and his two hundred soldiers, who were about to leave.

In addition to Thouar's account, Campos's writings and those of José Paz Guillén, a member of the expedition, are our main sources of information about this trip. I am relying primarily on the earliest accounts published by Thouar, in 1884: as we will see, his information, and especially his interpretation, changed considerably in his later writings.

More than a year after the massacre, Thouar had not learned much about Crevaux's death. He mentions the discovery of a plank from one of the boats at Cabayurepoti in September 1883, but this may be the same piece that was discovered several months earlier by the Rivas expedition. The other objects on Thouar's list were for the most part recovered by the missionaries before the 1883 expedition. In addition to the plank from the boat, Thouar recovered the following objects:
- a drawing of the Pilcomayo done by Crevaux
- Crevaux's letter to Giannecchini in which he gives him his mule
- the coins recovered at the San Francisco mission
- the barometer [or chronometer?] that Campos turned over to Thouar at Tarija

Thouar adds that an Indian had been seen several times in the vicinity of Itiyuru wearing one of the expedition's chronometers around his neck, "like an amulet"; another Indian had been seen wearing the frock coat belonging to Louis Billet, the astronomer accompanying Crevaux. Later, when Thouar had returned to France, the list of relics grew, first with Crevaux's gold-rimmed binoculars bearing the initials J. C., his surgeon's kit, a compass, some papers, and a little money. Still later, in the 1891 edition of his travel narrative, Thouar adds a few more objects:
- a parasol
- a drawing of the river at Tarija made by Auguste Ringel
- a letter from Ringel written to the San Francisco mission on April 19, 1882—in other words the day the expedition set out

- a letter from Ernest Haurat
- two letters from Crevaux, one addressed to M. Didelot in Paris and dated January 15, 1882. In reality, Thouar had found these two letters at the beginning of 1886 at Jujuy (where Crevaux had written them) when he passed through the town.

True, the list is long. But it does not contribute much to solving the mystery of the explorers' deaths. The information gathered in the course of the 1883 expedition is rather thin and boils down to a few dialogues between Thouar and the Teyu Tobas as the Bolivians were starting to establish the new settlement: "All of my efforts to recover the remains and the papers of the unfortunate doctor Crevaux from the Indians have been in vain"; "I had numerous interviews with the Tobas concerning the survivors, all of which were to no avail, these unfortunates having already been dead for a long time!"[29]

Much farther downstream, in a Toba camp near the Patiño Falls, Thouar momentarily thinks he has found the most valuable relic of all: "A human skull together with a few sun-bleached fragments of pelvic bone, attached to the top of this pole ... my heart was beating as though it would burst ... If it was him ... if it was one of them! I cut the pole down with my machete, I took the bones, which I hung on my saddle." Yet five months later, in Paris, an examination of these bones by Mr. de Quatrefages and Doctor Hamy revealed the skull to be that of a Toba Indian.[30]

Although his own text shows that he did not manage to discover anything else about the massacre of the Crevaux expedition, Thouar gained one certainty: he presents himself as a fervent defender of the Franciscan brothers (and of Giannecchini in particular), whom the settlers accused of having facilitated, or even planned, the murder. Thouar defends the missionaries tooth and claw. When he writes to the president of the Société de Géographie de Paris to appraise him of the true causes of Crevaux's death, he accuses the people of Caiza of having provoked the massacre with their expedition against the Noctenes, and he exclaims: "In the name of justice and truth, I declare that they [the Franciscans] are innocent of the crime they are accused of."[31] At the end of his account, he further affirms: "It is not the least of my satisfactions to think of the fate of these poor Italian missionaries, whose life, whose safety found themselves threatened by the most terrible accusation!"[32] In May 1886, having returned to Bolivia to mount a new expedition, he even told the Tarija College superintendent, a Franciscan, that he had asked

Figure 19. The Pilcomayo and the Crevaux Settlement
Teófilo Novis, *El Chaco en imágenes* ([1887] 2016), p. 126.

the French government to decorate Doroteo Giannecchini to show there was no doubt about his conduct.[33]

We will see that Thouar would change his mind substantially a few years later.

On August 29, 1883, the expedition led by Daniel Campos founded the Crevaux Settlement at Santa Bárbara de Teyu, so named in memory of the French explorer killed there. While the majority of the group continued on to the Paraguay, Doctor Gumercindo Arancibia, physician and official colonial agent, now in charge of the new foundation, stayed behind. Under his management and until September 1884, several episodes ensued which have to do with our story.

The first episode was "a memorable event: the discovery of Crevaux's skull," which occurred at the same time that Thouar, then farther downriver, thought he had found the same skull. In effect, on September 23, 1883, when he arrived to work on construction of the Settlement, some Chiriguano neophytes from Machareti announced that, on their way, they had found "a skull hanging in a tree, affirming that it belonged to Crevaux." The next day the grand captain of the Machareti people, Mandepora, left with fifteen men to cut it down:

At 1 p.m., this captain presented a human skull found in the place called Yanduyanca ("ostrich head"), on the big track upstream, two and a half leagues north of this Settlement, hanging from a tree called *tusca* [*Acacia aroma*], where it seems that the Tobas left it a short time ago, after celebrating the full moon. Local tradition affirms that, when the savages kill a headman or a great chief in the course of their thieving and murdering, they cut off his head and hang it from a tree in order to parade it through their villages every month when the moon is waxing.[34]

Arancibia adds that the Tobas probably abandoned the skull because they were convinced that "the colonization of the Pilcomayo began with the search for the mortal remains of the fearless Frenchman."

In his role as physician, Arancibia measured the skull, studied it, and concluded that it presented "the aspect and configuration of a skull of Caucasian race ... We can thus deduce that the skull is that of the late Dr. Jules Crevaux, which his country, his friends, and his family will soon receive from the Government to be placed in the sanctuary of science as a trophy of science's sacrifice to human progress." On October 17, the "sacred skull" arrived in Tarija, where the prefecture ordered that a solemn funeral be held. The inhabitants of the town demanded that the skull should be kept as a relic at Tarija, unless the French government requested its return.

Scarcely a month after these ceremonies, another skull became the center of an unfortunate episode at the Crevaux Settlement: it was that of the Toba, Cuserai. At the same time as the New Settlement was being founded, the Tobas, Cuserai and Peloco, had presented themselves to Daniel Campos, who had asked them to return the horses stolen from the Rivas expedition the previous year, but also to return Crevaux's belongings. Peloco seems to have been the father of Pelocolijiguaso, who, in June 1882, had sent his men to the San Francisco mission to negotiate the liberation of Francisco Zeballos. A short time later, in Cabayurepoti, Peloco offered his own sons to guide Campos and his soldiers as far as Piquirenda. Cuserai, we have already met. Campos describes him as an "Indian runaway from one of the missions and a sinister instigator of thefts and crimes."[35]

The new military settlement sealed the fate of this Toba whom many early witnesses identified as Crevaux's murderer. In the Franciscans' account of his death, a new toponym appears fleetingly in connection with the massacre of the Crevaux expedition. In November 1883, Cuserai and three companions arrived at the Settlement to return the horses.

In the meantime, other Tobas at Güiraitarenda, where Crevaux and his companions were murdered, were searching for and trying to recover the remains in order to return them to the Christians, as the men of the expedition had asked them. When the four Tobas mentioned got to the Settlement, the official agent turned a deaf ear and ordered the soldiers to open fire. The Tobas tried to flee by jumping into the river, but Cuserai, Autagaicoluqui, and one other perished under the Christian bullets, and only the fourth man, called Cutaicoliqui, managed to escape even though he was wounded. The corpse of the unfortunate Cuserai was savagely disemboweled and dismembered, and his head roasted and taken to Tarija. This happened in November; thus precisely ten years after the Tobas' stupid desertion, the two main authors died a horrible death at the same hour, even as they were seeking the peace they had not wanted to accept at the mission they had so ungratefully abandoned.[36]

Giannecchini's description is even more terrifying:

Cuserai jumped in the water to escape, they wounded him but he continued on, limping. The soldiers fired relentlessly but did not hit him. A Chiriguano from Machareti hit him in the thigh when he was getting out of the water on the other bank, and he fell. Arancibia immediately ordered him to be finished off, and they cut off his head. He was still alive, so they hit him on the head with a stick until he fainted. Afterward, Arancibia cut his throat with a knife, roasted his head, skinned it, discarded the flesh and carried off the skull. They opened his belly, his chest and his stomach, and with the ferociousness and enjoyment of hyenas, they made fun of him and, shouting the most obscene and repugnant words, they amused themselves by searching his bowels for the cows that had been stolen and eaten, the fish, the gold, Crevaux's money, etc.!!! They tore out all his intestines and left them for the vultures.[37]

Was Arancibia answering skull for skull? Whatever the case, the "Christians" and "civilized men" demonstrated on this occasion that their barbarism was a good match for that of the "savages," and that Cuserai's death had significant consequences: "The Tobas at Güiraitarenda discarded Crevaux's effects and resolved to take revenge. The official colonial agent, fearing that his acts of barbarism would be disapproved of by the Government, as in fact they were ... attempted to blame this cruel attack on our mission Indians, who were working as day laborers at the Settlement."[38]

At the beginning of 1884, a large army of Tobas, commanded by the survivor Cutaicoliqui—the same who, in July 1882, maintained his innocence in the death of Crevaux—made its way toward Aguairenda and Caiza, "wishing to unleash their hatred on the many inhabitants and cattle in the vicinity." However before reaching their destination, they encountered and attacked, not far from the Crevaux Settlement, a group of traveling Criollos; they stole their horses, killed four men, and captured a young bride, Cecilia Oviedo, and her little brother, Manuel.[39] There can be no doubt about it, the attack and the abduction were direct consequences of Cuserai's killing—"*legitimate* consequences of the death and betrayal of which Cuserai was victim," as Giannecchini puts it.[40] Freed six months later thanks to the Franciscans' intervention, Cecilia confirms this. In her account, we also find the young Yallá, peace ambassadress of the Crevaux expedition.

> I could not understand anything they were saying to me or their songs. But one Toba, Petrona Yallá, who spoke a little Spanish, told me that all these manifestations of victory and what they were saying to me were what mothers say to those who have killed their sons or their husbands; [she told me] that I had fallen into their hands in reprisal for the betrayal and killing of Cuserai and his companions when they came to negotiate with the soldiers of the Crevaux Settlement.[41]

Cecilia Oviedo's liberation was the opportunity seized upon by several Tobas, whose strength had been sapped by constant struggle against the Criollos, to sue for peace. On this occasion, Miguel Estenssoro, commander of the fort, asked the prefecture to send him two dozen knives, a dozen cotton ponchos ("the cheapest you can find"), four lengths of cloth, and a dozen wool hats "with colorful ribbons," such gifts being indispensable for making peace. Estenssoro added that, in these conditions, it would also be possible "to recover some of the effects stolen from Mr. Crevaux."[42]

Two months later, on September 14, 1884, the peace treaty was concluded at the San Francisco mission. The Indians were represented by fifteen Toba captains, four Noctenes, one "Tapiete," and three Chorotes.[43] The Tobas involved usually divided their time between the San Francisco mission and Cabayurepoti; among them were Caligagae, father of the

Figure 20. The Crevaux Settlement
Teófilo Novis, *El Chaco en imágenes* ([1887] 2016), p. 127.

young Yallá. The treaty also mentions a certain Poloco, interpreter, who was perhaps the Peloco we have already met. Conspicuously absent is Cutaicoliqui, the abductor of Cecilia and Cuserai's avenger.

A few years passed without major developments. The principal event came at the end of 1884: as another consequence of the treaty signed in September, the Tobas freed a *karai* they had been holding for many years, José Napoleón Correa. Depending on the author, Correa had been a prisoner of the Tobas for either fourteen, eighteen, or nineteen years. Others provide more details: on September 2, 1866, at the age of seven, José Napoleón was captured at the same time as his adoptive parents; the latter and a baby were set free in November of the same year thanks to the Franciscans, but not José, because the frontier settlers refused to free in exchange the son of a Toba headman, Cayutii. According to Corrado, writing in 1884, the young man raised by the Tobas "had adapted to them and their customs" and had several times refused to return to his people, preferring to live among the Tobas and as one of them."[44] It is not surprising, then, that according to a few authors, Correa was present at the massacre of the French expedition in

1882: as we will see, he adds some new information about the circumstances of the crime.

Two years later, in 1886, the Bolivian government decided to organize a new expedition in the Chaco. The objective was no longer Asunción or exploration of the Pilcomayo. It was Puerto Pacheco, on the Upper Paraguay, a Bolivian port founded in 1885 by the businessman (and explorer) Miguel Suárez Arana. This is the present-day Bahía Negra, which now belongs to Paraguay. The expedition was to leave from the region of Isoso, on the Parapeti River, locate and reclear, if necessary, the tracks cleared earlier by Antonio Rojas, Miguel Suárez Arana, and his son Cristián, to reach the salt flats of Chiquitos to the east and from there open a way as far as Puerto Pacheco.

In Buenos Aires, where he arrived after having explored the delta of the Pilcomayo on behalf of the Argentinian government, Thouar received an invitation from Bolivia to lead a new expedition. The documents show that Thouar was sent to Sucre by the Centro Boliviano of Buenos Aires to represent it in this new attempt.

Whatever the case may be, unlike the earlier Argentinian expeditions and Thouar's first voyage in 1883, the goal of the expedition that left for the Isoso region on December 2, 1886, was not to investigate Crevaux's death nor did it plan to go via the Pilcomayo. And yet not only did it take this route, but furthermore, the journey to the Pilcomayo in 1887 turned into yet another opportunity to gather new information about the French mission killings five years earlier. Indeed the Thouar of 1887 has much more to say about Crevaux than the Thouar who set out on his trail in 1883.

Two important figures for us were members of the expedition: Fr. Doroteo Giannecchini, the chaplain, whom we have already met; and the French artist Théophile/Teófilo Novis. In February 1886, Novis found himself at Tucumán, where he met Thouar, who was on his way to Sucre, and joined up with him. When the 1887 expedition was over, Novis returned to France with Thouar, and even married his sister, before returning to Bolivia at the end of the century. In France, and then in Sucre where he lived until his death, "Teófilo" Novis wrote several stories set in the Chaco Boreal. He called this series "Travel Memories," even though not all of the tales related true experiences: one example is a short account of the Crevaux expedition, in which the Alsatian artist had obviously not participated.

The two travelers arrived in Tarija on April 6 and spent nearly a month there, remaining until May 4. While they were there, Giannecchini

Figure 21. Émile Arthur Thouar
gallica.bnf-fr/Bibliothèque nationale de France.

entrusted Thouar with two relics: "Crevaux's skull," found in September of 1883, and that of Cuserai, duly roasted by Arancibia and kept in Tarija. Later Thouar took the two skulls back to France with him. Giannecchini added Crevaux's revolver and the striped jersey belonging to his helmsman, Haurat, which had been returned by the Tobas.

The travelers spent from May 16 to June 28 on the Chaco frontier, or more precisely in the Franciscan missions of the region. During this time, Thouar is reported to have made two interviews of great importance for the Crevaux affair: the first on May 18, with José Correa; the second between the 20th and the 27th of the same month with Yallá, the young peace ambassadress on the 1882 expedition, who was now living at the San Francisco mission.[45] Thouar records the meeting with Correa in his travel notes for May, but not that with Yallá: the notes indicate only one interview with "Pelokoliki" and several Toba "men and women."[46] Thouar does not mention either of the two interrogations in his later publications. José Correa does not appear at all, and the first encounter with Yallá is dated May 1887, in other words a year later.

Thouar and Novis then headed for Sucre, from where, after several months of preparation, the expedition finally left on December 2 for the Isoso region, where it failed lamentably to clear a path eastward. It was then that Thouar decided to strike out for Machareti to the south, and from there to the Pilcomayo, in order to reconnoiter possible ways of reaching Puerto Pacheco.

On this part of the journey, the inquiry into Crevaux's murder resumed. Thouar ordered two members of the expedition, the doctor, Nicolás Ortiz, and a certain José Portillo, to try to recover all possible information on the massacre. More importantly, Yallá reappears in the same part of the trip.

On May 20, 1887, Thouar traveled from the Machareti mission to the San Francisco mission, with the intention of gauging the Tobas' state of mind in preparation for his trip. There he met the "Indian Kaligagaë, the father of Yallá who played such a fatal role in the Crevaux massacre." Together with Novis, Thouar talked with the girl, not about the expedition preparing to set off, but about the one that had been massacred five years earlier. The young Indian ultimately gave up the names of the Tobas who had killed Crevaux: "She told me that Cuserai … was one of Crevaux's killers, and that the others who took part were Cototo, Suguai, Cutiguasu, Peloko, Tasikii, etc."[47]

A few days later, on June 3, Thouar met at Machareti with several Toba and "Tapiete" captains from downstream: in addition to Caligagae,

Figure 22. The murder of Dr. Crevaux
André Bresson, *Bolivia* (1886), p. 417.

who assured him that the Indians would not oppose the expedition's passage, Cutaicoliqui and Cototo were present, in other words, at least one of the purported killers denounced by Yallá.[48]

Thouar maintained that Yallá quickly gave him her full trust and the details of the massacre. According to him, she better remembered Ernest Haurat, who was thought to have survived his companions for some time. Thouar makes no allusion to the version then circulating about

Yallá's role in the (temporary) rescue of Haurat and another member of Crevaux's crew. Indeed, some believed that the two men were "saved first of all thanks to the tender and charitable influence of the Indian, Yallá, who spared them from death."49 Thouar speaks, by contrast, of Yallá's "fatal" role: she was reputedly the one who had warned the Pilcomayo Tobas of the French explorers' impending arrival.

But above and beyond this new information, the 1887 expedition also, or especially, marks a radical turning point in Thouar's assessment of the role played by the Franciscan missionaries in Crevaux's death: whereas a few years earlier, he staunchly defended their innocence, he was now transparently accusing Crevaux's mentor in the Bolivian Chaco, Doroteo Giannecchini. And that is what we will now examine.

CHAPTER 4

Imposture and Amnesia

A half century after Crevaux's death, a French traveler added a new element and revealed "Dr. Crevaux's last message." In the 1940s, Roger Courteville claimed to have found the last photos taken by Crevaux, hidden in a clay jar in the house of an old Toba sorcerer. He recognized them because on one of them was a man who looked very like Crevaux—and it was ... but in a photo taken much earlier, a studio photo later retouched and superimposed on another background. In yet another photo, Courteville claimed to recognize, sixty years later, his Toba sorcerer (who furthermore, he said, was the killer in person), whereas it was a photo of some Ticuna Indians in the Peruvian zone of Amazonia, taken in 1865 by the German traveler, Albert Frisch. This deception has recently been unmasked,[1] but not before it was repeated by several authors. It interests us here only because it was the last in a long series of unsubstantiated rumors, groundless information, dubious testimonies, and outright lies, which began immediately after Crevaux's death.

Nearly 150 years after the massacre, the evidence has disappeared, and it is no longer possible to question new witnesses. The material available to us now consists of reports and other texts written by early detectives on the Chaco border: newspaper articles, official reports, correspondence, and especially several books that were more widely diffused than the public or private documents. Indeed a number of works on the affair appeared: Giannecchini's *Diario* and his *Relación*, about the Crevaux and Rivas expeditions in 1882; Thouar's first account (1884);

books by Campos and Paz Guillén on the 1883 expedition as far as Asunción; Giannecchini's second *Diario*, about the 1887 expedition; and about the same expedition; Thouar's account published in 1889–1890. To these must be added Thouar's book, written in 1891, which gathers into a single volume his expedition reports for 1883 and 1887: on this occasion, as we will see, the explorer sometimes considerably alters his earlier reports.

All of the subsequent literature is based on these books and on the early lecture given by Vaca Guzmán in June 1882 in homage to Crevaux. Olaf Storm, for instance, borrows most of his information from Vaca Guzmán's lecture and from Paz Guillén's book, while volumes by the French authors Georges Frank, André Bresson, or Théophile Novis are based on Thouar's accounts. Thouar himself shamelessly plagarizes Giannecchini's text in several places, in particular for his description of preparations made for Crevaux's expeditions to Tarija and San Francisco. Very few of the texts add any new information in the following years and decades: a few isolated elements from the Argentinian side (Baldrich, Roldán, and then Wagner in 1910); bits of the Tarija tradition collected by Bernardo Trigo, and not much else.

Yet even though they were more closely involved in the Crevaux affair, none of the earliest authors was present on the banks of the Pilcomayo on that fateful April day in 1882. They, too, based their accounts on more direct sources, indications, and witnesses.

The earliest information that arrived at the Chaco border and, from there, reached the Bolivian, Argentinian, and French authorities resulted from questioning several Indians and Criollos who had either witnessed or taken part in the massacre.

By order of appearance, the list of witnesses is as follows:
- The first to appear was Yahuanahua, the Chiriguano Indian who had announced the killing to the authorities of Itiyuru and Caiza. He was questioned by Eudogio Raña, subprefect of Gran Chaco.
- Another Chiriguano involved was one of the survivors of the massacre: Iramaye, from the Tigüipa mission, who had accompanied the Crevaux mission as interpreter. Whether he was freed by the Tobas at the same time as Francisco Zeballos or he escaped on his own (the sources differ on this subject), Iramaye crops up at any rate again on the Chaco border. He was questioned by Felizardo Terceros in Caiza.
- In July 1882, another survivor, the young Zeballos, also gave his testimony, which was published in the local papers.

- The same month, the Toba headmen Caligagae, Iñiri, and Cutaicoliqui maintained their innocence at the San Francisco mission. In August, accompanied by Pelocoliqui-guazu, they reiterated their innocence to Giannecchini and to the subprefect of Gran Chaco.
- Other crucial testimony was provided by frontier settlers, like David Gareca or the Frenchman Milhomme, who in turn must have had their own sources of information. The letter dated June 8, 1882, written by a Franciscan, reported having "credible news" gathered "in Itiyuru and its vicinity."
- Finally in 1884, José Correa entered the picture, freed by the Tobas after long years in captivity.
- In 1887, the list of witnesses grew with the reappearance of Yallá, the young Toba sent as ambassadress to the Pilcomayo in 1882 and who had not returned: in 1887 she became Arthur Thouar's chief informant.

With this list of firsthand informants our problems begin. Each seems more unlikely than the next, and their "credible" testimonies cannot help but be affected.

Yahuanahua can be suspected of complicity: in effect, he could have been the "spy" who warned the Tobas that the Crevaux mission was coming. Eudogio Raña, who questioned him, had his doubts: although Yahuanahua claimed to have arrived at the scene of the crime after the killings, "what he says suggests he was present."[2]

Likewise, Iramaye's role (or the simple fact that he survived) made him suspect in the eyes of the frontier settlers. Indeed if the Tobas who arrived at the San Francisco mission in June offered to free a so-called captive Iramaye, the story changed shortly afterward, and Fr. Marcelleti warned Eudogio Raña that "the little Indian from Tigüipa deliberately chose to remain among the wicked men of Teyu."[3]

A year on, Campos, who was preparing to explore the Pilcomayo, wrote to Esteban Castillo, corregidor, or magistrate, of Ñancaroinza:

> The present superintendence has learned that the neophyte who accompanied the unfortunate Crevaux expedition as interpreter is in the area; as it is indispensable to investigate the above-named interpreter, I am applying to you to use all means and, in agreement with the local authorities, to have him escorted to me under guard, who will be paid here, giving the Indian to understand that we simply want to ask him to clear up a few things, without worrying him.[4]

Figure 23. "José Correa, Bolivian. Held captive by the Tobas for 19 years. Born in Caiza"
Drawing by Théophile Novis (Archives Nationales, F/17/3009B, dossier Thouar).

Why an escort if Iramaye has nothing to worry about? And in fact, he did become frightened and remained in hiding. Fr. Santiago Romano, who was in charge of the Machareti mission, wrote on this occasion to Giannecchini that the Caiza settlers claimed it was the missionaries who were hiding the interpreter, "so that he would not reveal that we had been complicit in Crevaux's death."[5]

Iramaye and Yahuanahua could just as well have been innocent as actually involved in the death: in either case we are allowed to doubt their credibility, whether they were lying or defending themselves by accusing others.

Francisco Zeballos's case is different, but more disturbing. When he was freed after two months of captivity and having witnessed the massacre, Francisco was "greatly affected and nearly beside himself."[6] Daniel Campos assures that he was recovered "in a lamentable state of mental fragility" and, to stimulate him, on June 20, 1883, Campos appointed him second lieutenant of the Potosi squadron. According to Campos, "this act of strict justice, though belated, produced a strong moral reaction in the young soldier; he visibly recovered his memory and intelligence, which had been as though extinguished by his past misfortunes and the injustice of which he had been a victim."[7] But not everyone was of the same opinion: "In 1896, I saw him at Potosi; the poor wretch did not remember a thing"; "Young Zeballos was fourteen or fifteen when his father was killed before his eyes. The poor boy was half crazed when I saw him in 1869 [sic, 1896] at Potosi."[8] Above and beyond the trauma, Francisco was not the key witness we might imagine: "He did not know the names of the places they had passed through; he spoke none of the Indian languages; to which can be added his fear, altogether natural given his situation, and the particular care the Tobas took to keep their secrets from him."[9]

The two Chiriguano suspects and an amnesiac survivor, traumatized or uninformed, are joined by the Toba captains questioned at the San Francisco mission by Fr. Marcelleti. Caligagae and his colleagues defended themselves by offering up other culprits: in July it was the Tobas downriver from Cabayurepoti, or the Güisnays of Sirome; in August it was the Noctenes; the travelers' money was in Itiyuru and their weapons in Piquirenda. If Iramaye and Yahuanahua were suspected of complicity, the Tobas on the other hand were directly accused of the crime. True or false, their information was above all a desperate attempt to defend themselves and therefore hardly credible. As the editorialist, Luis Paz, notes, the Indians' declarations had "as sole objective to excuse themselves and accuse each other."[10]

The frontier Criollos were also on the defensive, and especially those in Caiza, organizers of the March 1882 expedition which, in the missionaries' version, was the cause of the Indians' revenge on Crevaux. Furthermore the settlers, whose friends and relatives were members of Crevaux's crew, were drunk with vengeance. Their testimonies stress above all the Tobas' extraordinary cruelty, or even Crevaux's naivety for having trusted the Indians and dismissed their own words of warning. Nor did they hesitate to attribute what had happened to a sinister Franciscan influence among the Pilcomayo Indians. Several of the letters written on the frontier and published in the Tarija papers were anonymous as well.

The case of José Correa is just as problematic. The young man had been "liberated" in 1884, but, if we are to believe Fr. Corrado, he lived freely among the Tobas and as one of them. The ex-captive first gave his testimony to someone who lived in Caiza, whose letter was published in the newspaper *El Trabajo* on December 22, 1885. He was next questioned by Thouar in May 1886.11 According to the letter published in the Tarija newspaper, Correa had lived with the Tobas so long that he had forgotten his Spanish. It was indeed in Guarani, through an interpreter, that Thouar questioned him in 1886. And if, in 1885, he claimed to have witnessed Crevaux's death at first hand, a year later he maintained the opposite. That did not stop Thouar from repeating in 1906 that "Correa, a Bolivian subject ... was present when Crevaux was massacred."12 It is extremely difficult, not to say impossible, to determine how much truth there is in Correa's contradictions (and/or of those who reported his words), and to separate this from a possible desire for sensationalism or, who knows, an effort to keep his true role in the massacre of the French expedition a secret.

Our list of eyewitnesses ends with Yallá, who deserves a separate mention. Her case, in effect, is intertwined with that of the "French impostor," Arthur Thouar.

In 1883, with the relative success of the Campos expedition, which, without having actually managed to clear a stable route to the Paraguay, nevertheless got as far as Asunción, Thouar had reached the peak of his professional career as an explorer. The Thouar myth was beginning to superimpose itself, in a certain fashion, on that of Crevaux. When he returned to France, the Société de Géographie awarded him their gold medal for his journey in the footsteps of Crevaux. Homages and congratulations flowed in from all around. A few did not hesitate to improve on the truth and claim that Thouar had just returned to France from a trip to South America when the news of the massacre exploded, and he "had decided to go back to clear up the mystery"13—we know in point of fact that he was in Santiago de Chile and had been sent to Bolivia by the French authorities. Better yet, forgetting about Campos and his two hundred soldiers, others or the same maintained that the explorer had set out alone for the Pilcomayo, that he had refused an escort, that he had gone alone into the Chaco—if the truth be told, Thouar himself scarcely mentions his large escort in his books and even later claims that he set out alone and "without means" in 1883.14

On the Bolivian side, Thouar was the hero of the hour. The government offered the direction of the new expedition slated for 1887 "to the intelligent and enterprising explorer," to "the intrepid" Thouar.[15] Nor did the Franciscan brothers in Tarija stint in their praise for "the wise explorer of the Pilcomayo" who had defended them so well in 1883; one of them, perhaps Fr. Pifferi, even dedicated a poem to him.[16] But the idyll was not long lived.

Already in 1883, a few discordant voices could be heard rising from the concert of praise for Thouar. David Gareca, a Caiza settler who had taken part in the Campos expedition (and the year before that in the expedition led by the Criollos of Caiza shortly before Crevaux arrived), criticized him for his obstinate refusal to follow the Indian guides, and even accused him of intending to abandon the bulk of the party and set out on a one-man "traitor's march." For Gareca, this "French impostor" was merely "seeking his own glory."[17] Even Daniel Campos, who in the beginning could not have enough praise for this "distinguished explorer," this "enterprising warrior spirit," with whom he was united by "a close, fraternal friendship,"[18] later changed his tune. In fact, once he had reached Asunción, Thouar accused Campos of having tried to have him killed; he also took all the credit for the expedition that had in reality been led by Campos. The accusations went no further, and Thouar was obliged to retract them,[19] but the harm was done. Campos enthusiastically published the denunciation of the Centro Boliviano of Buenos Aires, which had paid for Thouar's trip to Sucre in 1886 so that he might explore the Chaco on behalf of the Center: the only thing the Centro Boliviano obtained was that, when he got to Sucre, Thouar canceled his membership, before the expedition even began. The Bolivians of Buenos Aires were indignant and published a "Manifesto against Mr. Arturo Thouar" in which they described him as a "clever plagiarist of scientific studies done by others," and published several letters from Campos on "this icily perverse [man, who] is not fated, no, is not fated to die righteously" and who in 1886, "was received like a god at Sucre, where he had duped everyone."

These voices multiplied after the resounding failure of Thouar's new expedition in 1887. From February 3 to May 9, the explorers camped at Carumbey, in the Isoso region, on the banks of the Parapeti River, looking to open a route that would lead to the Chiquitos salt flats and from there to Puerto Pacheco. From the banks of the Parapeti, Thouar could see a hill, which he identified as the Mount San Miguel that overlooks the Chiquitos salt flats; in reality it was Mount Curundaití, "which he carelessly took for San Miguel on no other basis than a vague resemblance to a drawing of the real San Miguel that Mr. Cristián Suárez Arana had given him. This error was the direct cause of the expedition's failure." In effect, because he saw Mount San Miguel there where it was not, Thouar maintained that the breach Suárez Arana had opened earlier lay in the wrong direction and therefore he did not attempt to reach it. Furthermore, whereas his identification of Mount San Miguel promised a relatively rapid, safe journey to the salt flats, "the strangest, most incomprehensible thing" was that, instead of taking this route, Thouar decided to explore the Parapeti lowlands to the north. This "reconnaissance tour, undoubtedly of geographical interest … did not figure among his attributions."[20]

Thouar sent a commission to Chiquitos (via Santa Cruz), which he tasked with establishing the authenticity of Mount San Miguel. When they returned to report that they could only confirm that the explorer had been mistaken in his claims, Thouar did not bat an eye and concluded that there were "two hills bearing the name San Miguel."[21] At the same time, he began developing a "very strange idea," namely that the Chaco Boreal was located at one degree longitude less than what was shown on the map made by John Minchin in 1879, regarded as the most reliable at the time.[22] Neither this conclusion nor efforts to identify the hills appeared in Thouar's published accounts: there, for the benefit of his French readers, the imperturbable explorer continued to scale mount "San Miguel-Curundaiti." But he did not find his way for all that.

Thouar therefore decided to switch directions and to set off to the south, for the French mission of Machareti. From there, the right direction for Puerto Pacheco lies to the northeast, but the explorer chose to make for the Crevaux Settlement, in other words to the southeast, following a "winding and unexpected route": "The Information Commission considers the southeasterly direction taken by Mr. Thouar to be an unsolvable riddle." Next the explorer took a northerly and even northwesterly route from the Crevaux Settlement, such that, weaving back and forth, "according to the expedition members heard by the Commission, the Indians said that the path they followed ended up back in the Isoso region."[23]

These errors could have been corrected by the Indian guides, but Arthur Thouar did not trust them any more than he had in 1883 and, consequently, did not heed their advice. After so many orders and counterorders, no one was surprised when, on August 10, Thouar separated from the main body of the party. "He abandoned us," Giannecchini writes.[24] The story ends when Thouar and his last three companions (among whom was Novis) are finally rescued, half dead from thirst, hunger, and exhaustion, by Colonel Martínez, who arrived via Caiza and the Crevaux Settlement.

The unanimity against Thouar was overwhelming. In addition to Giannecchini and the Information Commission (put together precisely because of the amount of criticism at the end of the expedition), many others protested the Frenchman's actions. After his departure on August 10, the members of the expedition elected Doctor Nicolás as "interim leader," and all signed the following act:

Consequent upon the conduct of Mr. Thouar, who abandoned his post and disappointed the members of the expedition, deserting them with premeditation and without asking the opinion of those who had followed him or of those who had remained in camp; having sent, to arrive at his ends, a group to the Crevaux Settlement: we have decided to express a protest that shows the Government and the country the indignation such behavior has aroused in us.[25]

That very day, Ortiz wrote to the Government to report that "Mr. Thouar's secret departure" casts doubt on "the morality of his actions" and evokes "the leader who has abandoned his post, has quit the common flag, perhaps in search of shinier laurels that, selfishly, he wants to gather for himself alone."[26]

Thouar's predecessors in the Chaco had the same reactions. Cristián Suárez Arana notes "the serious geographical error" made by a Thouar "completely disoriented in his calculations" about Mount San Miguel, and adds that "to take Machareti, near the Pilcomayo, as the starting point for opening the way to Puerto Pacheco was a lamentable absurdity."[27] John Minchin, author of the map criticized by Thouar, published a furious letter to the explorer in a Sucre newspaper, in which he sharply upbraided him for his unforgiveable "geographical error."[28] Olaf Storm, who in 1885 had already spoken of the "elementary astronomical errors" made by Thouar in the Pilcomayo delta, also casts doubt on his competence.[29]

To justify his failures and salve his wounded pride, Thouar hurls accusations right and left. The failure in the Isoso is first imputed to a lack of water; then it is due to the ill will of the region's Criollos, to that of the people of Santa Cruz, who are opposed to the Sucre government; Suárez Arana got the wrong trail, and Minchin got the longitude wrong by a degree. But the explanation he finally presented to the Bolivian government was that a route that went through the Isoso would favor the Department of Santa Cruz to the detriment of Sucre.[30] Clearly it was not one of the explorer's functions to pronounce on internal Bolivian political affairs, and the Commission formed to look into the sorry result of the expedition made no mistake about it: "One may believe that the leader, overwhelmed by his absolute disorientation, attempted to impute his fantastical imaginings to the ones or the others."[31]

But it is a fact that, above and beyond the recalcitrant Criollos and incompetent predecessors, Arthur Thouar's preferred culprits were the Pilcomayo Indians and the Franciscan missionaries. More specifically, they were the Tobas and Doroteo Giannecchini. While four years earlier Thouar had presented himself as a fervent defender of the friars, now he was accusing them. He ascribed the failure of his expedition to a plot on the part of Giannecchini and the Pilcomayo Tobas to kill him as they were believed to have killed Crevaux—"a fresh betrayal," "another crime," "in the silence of the desert."[32] Thouar maintained that it was for this reason that he had abandoned his men.

To demonstrate that Giannecchini and the Tobas were guilty in 1887, he had first to prove that they were guilty in the Crevaux affair in 1882. For that, Thouar began by peppering his 1889–1890 texts and his book written in 1891 with insidious allusions to the sinister friar. That is where Yallá comes in.

Thouar had not known the young Toba in 1883. In his first account of this expedition, when he mentions Yallá, he is translating Giannecchini's text into French, and, like the Franciscan, simply says that the girl did not reappear after she was sent to the Pilcomayo. When he republished his text in his 1891 book, things had changed substantially. A first commentary crops up when he talks about the meeting between Yallá and Crevaux. Thouar writes in 1891, but not in 1884: "The girl, it was later learned, had reluctantly left the house in Tarija where she was in service."[33] In 1899 he goes further, saying that "Yallá did not give into the threat of force."[34] In 1891 Thouar also adds a few paragraphs to his 1884 text. It is easier to appreciate the difference if we compare the different versions:

"A la recherche," 1884, p. 229 [Almost literal translation of Giannecchini, "Relación de lo obrado," pp. 639–40]	Text added by Thouar in 1891, here in bold (*Explorations*, p. 38)
"And if I die," he [Crevaux] said, "I die! But if you risk nothing, you will discover nothing and you will stay in the dark!" He hoped the Indian Yallá would return with her parents and the Indian captains, for he heartily wished to know what the Tobas thought: but his hope was unfounded … Petrona did not return at the appointed time!!	"If I have to die, I will die, but if you risk nothing, you will discover nothing and you will stay in the dark!" Petrona did not reappear at the appointed time.
	Doctor Crevaux did not pay sufficient heed to this circumstance, which should have warned him against the Indians' misleading promises. Moreover the exchange of dialogue between the Tobas and the girl would leave no doubt as to the premeditated character of the crime and the fatal role played by the Indian girl. **"Some *gringos carayes* [Christian foreigners] are soon to be coming on the Pilcomayo," she said. "They are going to the Paraguay. After them will come others who will occupy the river, and you will no longer be able to fish."** **—How many are they? The Tobas asked.** **Drawing as many little lines in the sand as there were members of the mission, Yallá thus told them there were twenty-one of them.**

	—Are there any *cuicos* (Bolivian soldiers)? —No. —Do they have weapons? —Yes! But they won't use them. They are *gringos muy sonsos* [very stupid foreigners]!" On April 13, in the company of Fr. Doroteo and the Bolivian delegate, he set out to investigate the Pirapo Falls … **two leagues upstream from the mission …**
On April 13, in the company of Fr. Doroteo and the Bolivian delegate, he set out to investigate the Pirapo Falls …	

A first hypothesis could be that the details of this dialogue were communicated to Thouar by Yallá herself (who else could know them?) and that he therefore added them in his 1891 edition. Whatever the case, the new version does not admit hesitation: Yallá is guilty, she is directly responsible for the murder of the Crevaux mission. That lends credibility to her revelations about the massacre; Yallá appears in Thouar's text as a credible witness—and therefore we cannot cast doubt on the accusations she repeatedly levels against Doroteo Giannecchini.

After the first conversation at the San Francisco mission, others occurred as the 1877 mission made its way, which the Indian girl seems to have followed alone and on her own. Each meeting took place in an isolated spot, in private and under cover of night; each time, Yallá relentlessly warned Thouar that the Tobas were lying in wait, ready to kill him. Each appearance of the girl coincided with increasingly clear accusations leveled at the Franciscans in general and Giannecchini in particular, which Thouar seasons with transparent allusion to Crevaux's tragic end.

Already the first interview at the San Francisco mission had been momentarily interrupted "by the arrival of two Chiriguanos, whom she told me were spies sent by the Father." In effect, Thouar goes on, her visit seemed to "have bothered [Fr. Giannecchini] a great deal."[35] Later, in Teyu where Thouar was interviewing Yallá again, Giannecchini encountered a Toba Indian and greeted him: "Without the slightest shame, he confessed that those savages who had been spying on us, who had stolen our animals and deserted and betrayed us were Indians known to him and over whom he had influence"; "I seemed to see, on this same beach

Figure 24. Conversation between Thouar and Yallá
Drawing by Riou from a sketch by Arthur Thouar, in Thouar, "Voyage dans le Chaco Boreal – 2" (1890), p. 183.

where, five years earlier, Crevaux and his companions had been heinously murdered, the corpse of our fellow countryman rise up between the missionary and the Tobas, perhaps one of the murderers."[36] Allusions proliferate in the pages that follow. After the scene at Teyu, when the Caiza settlers who were with the expedition became wary of Giannecchini, they also blamed Thouar for "being as blind as Crevaux, who would not listen to anyone"; when the Tobas were preparing to attack in August, "emissaries from the missions went around their tribes and incited them to fight!"; and when, finally, Colonel Martínez announced he was going to look for Thouar, at the end of September, it was reportedly another Franciscan, Fr. Sebastián Pifferi, who attempted to dissuade him by all possible means.[37]

Whoever reads Thouar's text and, more particularly, compares his different publications, can have no doubts. In the bitter words of Giannecchini, Thouar wanted to "place the responsibility for the horrible crime on the missionary Fathers and in particular on myself, perhaps not as its authors, but at least as direct accomplices."[38] Indeed, on the way back to Sucre in December 1887, Thouar and the two other Franciscans from the expedition (Noël Prat, who lived at Tomina, and Novis) did not hesitate to malign the Franciscans and to claim that "the Fathers were the cause of Crévat's [*sic*] death."[39]

Arthur Thouar did not succeed, and his accusations came to nothing. The outcome of the 1887 expedition also saw the end of the Thouar myth, which had sprung up four years earlier. His legend survived longer in France, but there, too, it finally faded away. In 1899, in a report to the French government and perhaps precisely because his glory had collapsed and his career come to a halt, the fallen explorer repeated his accusations, but to no more effect.

The threats from the Tobas and their Franciscan accomplices in 1887 were not only for Thouar a way to justify his failure: they were also, or above all, a remake of the Crevaux story. It is true that, if we compare Thouar's accounts of the various expeditions, he seems to have been much more interested in Crevaux's fate in 1887 than in 1883, although the purpose of his trip then was to investigate the crime. By 1899, he was claiming that he had begun to suspect Giannecchini after his first interview with Yallá in May 1886, in other words well before he set out on his second expedition. But neither his notes nor his book mentions this interview; in these texts, he first met Yallá only a year later, in May 1887, when the Thouar expedition was already in fairly rough shape after having failed in the Isoso. As others have already pointed out, throughout his career, Thouar wanted to appear as Crevaux's successor.[40] As early as 1884, he ended his account, exclaiming:

> Belonging to a Society [la Société de Géographie de Paris] that is highly honored in South America, was it not necessary to affirm that, there where one of the members succumbs, another presents himself? ... and this scrap of cloth, lacerated and stained, that Crevaux's hand, already in chill death, clutched in a final spasm, in a last contraction, did it not have to be collected? Did this not have to be done by a Frenchman?[41]

Shortly afterward, when it came time to explore the mouth of the Pilcomayo on behalf of Argentina, he writes that "The work of Dr. Crevaux is finally about to receive its first reward."[42] As he begins the 1887 expedition, he also evokes Crevaux's memory—but to say that he has surpassed him: "More fortunate than he, in 1883, at the head of a Bolivian column, I succeeded in the exploration in which he and his companions had so fatally succumbed."[43]

To consolidate his role as successor, what better than to get himself nearly (only nearly) massacred by the same Indians, and with the complicity of the same missionary? Thouar makes this clear in 1899, writing that "the revelation" of Giannecchini's guilt obliterated him: "Unfortunate Crevaux! Poor comrades! Fallen under the blows of a fierce hatred of civilization. *Will it not be my turn tomorrow?*"[44]

That is where Yallá comes in, whose presence is the obligatory connection between the Indians' threats, the Franciscans, Crevaux's tragic death, and Thouar's destiny.

That the Indian girl really existed is undeniable. She was a servant in Tarija, she left as ambassadress in 1882, and she never returned. That is all we know about her with any certainty in 1882. Her first attested interview with Thouar, in May 1887 at the San Francisco mission, was probably held in the place and at the date indicated—we know that Yallá's father was at the mission at that time and that he had met Thouar in Machareti on June 3. But the first purported meeting in May 1886 and the other interviews in 1887 on the banks of the Pilcomayo, under cover of night and without witnesses, are less sure. Very probably these conversations took place only in Thouar's imagination. The story told by the explorer is in effect hard to swallow. When Yallá revealed that the Tobas who met with Thouar at Machareti were those who were plotting to kill him, she would have been accusing her own father, who was present; the girl's many warnings of an Indian ambush always "farther downstream" and always "for tomorrow" are not credible either, and the threat never played out. We have trouble imagining hundreds of Indians patiently waiting for days on end for the moment to kill a handful of exhausted explorers dying of thirst in the desert—nor can we understand how so many Indians could have found water there where the explorers had not found a single drop. Finally it is frankly impossible that, as Thouar maintains, Yallá could have been at the Crevaux Settlement and asked a Choroti Indian to guide Colonel Martínez and, at the same time, have lent herself to a nocturnal interview with the explorer several days' walk distant.

There can be no doubt. The figure of Yallá who, like a protecting shadow, hovers throughout Thouar's book, was introduced by him to lend consistency to threats that, without her, would have lacked all credibility. Part of this construction was the 1891 modification of the text first published in 1884. Thouar does not change a comma in his fervent defense of the Franciscans and insists, even in 1891, that he has "always" defended Giannecchini. His later accusations cannot therefore be ascribed to an already existing prejudice; in 1883 Thouar appears as confident as Crevaux in 1882, but he then shows more cunning by revealing the Franciscan "plot."

In his 1891 edition, however, he adds some comments that are compromising for Giannecchini and, in particular, the paragraphs that unambiguously prove Yallá's betrayal. These lines show the Toba girl to be the indisputable traitor in 1882. For the same reason, Thouar does not mention her possible role in saving Blanco and Haurat: a Yallá guilty of treachery in 1882 is a much more reliable witness in 1887, and her revelations about Crevaux's death cannot be disputed—no more than her denunciation of a plot against Thouar.

The case of the "French impostor" is certainly the most notorious or at least the clearest, but, one way or another, all of our firsthand sources suffer from the same problem of credibility. There where Thouar lies and kills off a half-invented Yallá, Giannecchini writes explicitly to defend her. When he publishes his journal of the disastrous Rivas expedition of 1882, the friar unambiguously declares:

> The gratuitous slander that has circulated about my active and disinterested cooperation in the great undertaking to explore the Paraguay via the Pilcomayo; the official letter from the prefect of this department addressed to my respectable prelate and published in number 197 of *La Estrella de Tarija*; the letters, anonymous or not, that were sent to many places from the frontier after the failure of the expedition; and, finally, the insinuations by persons to whom I owe respect and deference, force me to publish my *Journal* in order to uphold, not my personal honor, but that of the venerable community to which I belong.[45]

History repeats itself when the Franciscan later publishes his journal of the 1887 expedition: faced with accusations by the people of Caiza in 1882 and by Thouar in 1887, Giannecchini defends and justifies himself, excuses when and as he can the Indians, and reproaches the Criollos for their cruelty. The latter counterattack and sow doubt as to the Franciscans' true role in Crevaux's murder. Furthermore all are writing after the events: Crevaux's murder is a chronicle of an announced murder, full of dark predictions and fatal forebodings.

Such are our firsthand sources, and such are our witnesses and suspects: demented, forgetful, and always contradictory. Such is the material evidence we have at our disposal and with which we must now work.

CHAPTER 5

Unresolved Questions

If the investigations following Crevaux's murder managed to gather certain details, they also left some questions unresolved or, on the contrary, with too many answers. The only way we can reopen the investigation today is to examine the early data once more, even if, in the welter of contradictory information that surfaces, the only hard fact seems to be the certainty that the French expedition was indeed massacred.

The least disputed fact is the date of the crime. And yet several versions circulated in the days following the murder: they diverge on the exact date, but also, oddly enough, on the rather insignificant point of the time of day. In May 1882, Martín, a Criollo from Yacuiba, gives April 25 as the date of the killing.[1] At the end of the month, the telegram sent by the subprefect of Tupiza, Francisco Arraya, to the Argentinian newspaper *La Nación* reports that "the catastrophe happened at the place called Tello on April 24 at 6:00 p.m." The latter date was adopted in the first instance by the Argentinian Geographical Institute and by the French representative in Buenos Aires, Mr. de Vienne. Following the report Vienne sent to Paris on June 5, the date of April 24 prevailed for a time in France.

But a short time later, the Franciscan author of the letter dated June 8, 1882, writes that "it is believed" that the crime took place on April 26 or 27 at ten in the morning. A few days later, the correspondent of the newspaper *El Trabajo* maintains that the explorers died on the fourth day of their trip, which would make the date April 23.[2]

April 27 is established as the date thanks to the later testimony (in July) of Francisco Zeballos, but the time changes: Crevaux now died at noon.[3] In his 1884 text, Thouar accepts this date, which is no longer seriously in question, but changes the time of death back to ten in the morning.[4] For the rest, neither the place, nor the killers' *modus operandi*, nor even the number of victims (not to mention possible survivors) garners a consensus.

Curiously there are few written sources that list with any precision the members of the Crevaux expedition. I found only two in the published texts, one reported by Vaca Guzmán and the other by Bernardo Trigo.

The victims were French, Argentinian, Bolivian … and Indian, which the documents of the time do not count as "Bolivians." Only much later, when the border conflict with Paraguay escalated, did the Indians begin to be considered (because they were needed to fight) as fully fledged citizens. By contrast, in 1882 the obedient mission neophytes and the unsubjugated barbarians of the Pilcomayo are merely Indians, and only Indians.

In the oldest sources, the number of members of the Crevaux expedition varies considerably, and the same contradictions appear again in the texts by Novis and Bernardo Trigo, written later but by persons with "firsthand" information—the first accompanied Thouar on the Pilcomayo, and the second had access to the records and traditions of Tarija. Table 1 sums up the information available:

Summing up: not only do the sources differ among themselves, but worse, the same author, Thouar, gives two different figures in the two texts. If he had forgotten to count the Argentinian members in 1884, he nevertheless mentions them in his account; in other words, he knew they existed. It comes as no surprise, then, that, given these contradictory figures, the confusion has only grown in the more recent publications. In 1999, Numa Broc's dictionary gives a total of fourteen expedition members killed: five Frenchmen and "their Bolivian guides."[5] In 1971, one study on the explorers of Bolivia first mentions no fewer than thirty-five persons: five Frenchmen, two Argentinians, eleven Criollo volunteers from Tarija, and "sixteen more expedition members in addition to Irimaya [*sic*] the interpreter." And even if the author maintains that Francisco Zeballos was the sole survivor, that does not prevent him going on to count only twenty-one killed: the five Frenchmen, fourteen

Table 1. Number of Members in the Crevaux Mission
(F: French; A: Argentinians; B: Bolivians; I: Indians)

Date	Author	Expedition members					Reference
		F	A	B	I	Total	
March 9, 1882	Samuel Campero, Prefect of Tarija					18	Letter to the Interior Minister, Tarija, March 9, 1882, ABNB MI 214/16
March 23, 1882	El Trabajo	5	2	14		21	El Trabajo, March 23, 1882, p. 3
April 17, 1882	J. Crevaux	5	2	9	1	17	Letter to the Finance Minister (Ministerio de hacienda de Bolivia), p. 46
May 11, 1882	El Trabajo	4 (5)	2	9		15 (16)	El Trabajo, May 11, 1882, p. 4*
June 8, 1882	A Franciscan	(no details)				15	Vaca Guzmán, El Esplorador, pp. 42–43
June 30, 1882	Vaca Guzmán	5	2	8	1	16	Vaca Guzmán, El Esplorador, pp. 37–38
July 24, 1882	Institut Géographique Argentino	(no details)				19	Sinval, Les Pionniers, p. 267
1884	Thouar	5	—	14	2	21	Thouar, "A la recherche," p. 230
1906	Thouar	5	2	16		23	Thouar, "Sur les bords du Pilcomayo. Massacrés par les Tobas," p. 55
1918	Novis	5	2	14		21	Novis, "Recuerdos," p. 343
1934	B. Trigo	5	2	16	1	24	B. Trigo, Las Tejas, pp. 194–95

* *El Trabajo* lists only four French members. I have added the fifth in parentheses because this is clearly an omission on the part of the paper, which knew full well that there were five Frenchmen. In fact, on page 2 of the same issue, *El Trabajo* mentions sixteen travelers in all.

Bolivians, and two Indian interpreters, whereas he listed only one in the beginning.[6] And I could go on.

Clearly the most reliable information should be that provided by Crevaux himself, which indicated a total of seventeen persons. But another clue could raise doubts. Two days after Crevaux's letters, the French artist, Auguste Ringel, also wrote a letter from the San Francisco mission, on the day of their departure, in which he reports that "a few Bolivians ran out on us."[7] And since Ringel gives neither the number of travelers who finally left nor whether the desertion took place before or after April 17, when Crevaux wrote his own letters, doubt persists: seventeen persons, with or without deserters? In all events, this illustrates a lack of enthusiasm on the part of the Criollos for this type of exploration, which entails leaving behind their families, their homes, and their activities, with no reward in sight. Subsequent expeditions encountered the same problem. In 1883, "there were very few people in Caiza. Some were on their farms; others had left upon hearing of our arrival, having been burned by previous experiences." "The recruiting plan I had set in place, according to my instructions, to swell the troops failed to produce good results. The people in these places run away and avoid helping us by all means available, either owing to the previous failures or because of the ill-treatment they have received on these expeditions, according to what they say."[8] In 1887 at Lagunillas, Thouar sent two officers to "incorporate the eleven nationals we need; at the last minute, there were hesitations: we were eager to sign the engagement, but, on the day of departure, they pleaded *un tío, una tía, mi caballito, mi vaquita!* (an uncle, an aunt, my horse, my cow!); we will come along *mañana* (tomorrow)."[9]

Even if, as Campos suggests, the memory of the tragic fate of the Crevaux mission or of the disaster of the Rivas expedition may have played a role in this reticence, the desertions in April 1882 show that this was not the only reason. Clearly the settlers did not really want to enter the Chaco, where they would face thirst, fatigue, and Indians.

Beyond confusion as to the number of the members of the Crevaux mission, there is also the question of their names. The two lists published by Vaca Guzmán and Bernardo Trigo repeat those published by the newspaper *El Trabajo* on two occasions: on March 23 and on May 11, 1882, in other words before and after the explorers' deaths. Bernardo Trigo based his list on that published in March, although he added other names as well; Vaca Guzmán, on the other hand, reproduced the May list. The two do not correspond exactly.

Table 2. Members of the Crevaux Mission

El Trabajo, March 23, 1882	B. Trigo, *Las Tejas*, pp. 194–95	*El Trabajo*, May 11, 1882 (reproduced in Vaca Guzmán, *El Esplorador*, pp. 37–38)
Argentinians: Blanco Carmelo, sailor Enrique Rodríguez, sailor	**Argentinians:** Carmelo Blanco, sailor Enrique Rodríguez, sailor	**Argentinians:** Blanco Carmelo Enrique Rodríguez
Frenchmen: Jules Crevaux, physician first class Louis Billet, astronomer Ernest Haurat, helmsman Jean Dumigron, assistant Auguste Kingel [*sic*], painter	**Frenchmen:** Julio Creveaux [*sic*], naval physician Luis Billet, astronomer Ernesto Huarat [*sic*], helmsman Jean Dumigrón [*sic*], assistant Augusto Kingel [*sic*], painter	**Frenchmen:** Julio Crevaux Luis Billet Ernesto Haurat Jean Dumigrón
Indians: ---	**Indians:** Iramaye	**Indians:** Iramaye, Indian interpreter
Bolivians from Tarija: Demócrito Cabezas, prefecture delegate Tomás Molina, secretary Baldomero Vera, captain Bernardino Valverdi, lieutenant Julián Romero Jacinto Gaiti Benjamín Roca, sub-lieutenant Sinforiano Velásquez Bernardo Civila Hermenejildo [*sic*] Dávila Francisco Arce Mariano Dolz Benigno Cardozo, aide-de-camp to delegate Lorenzo Vera, assistant *ad honorem*	**Bolivians from Tarija:** Baldomero Vera, captain Bernardino Valverde, lieutenant Julián Romero, détaché Jacinto Gaite, détaché Benjamín Roca, sub-lieutenant Sinforiano Velásquez Bernardo Sivila Hermenejildo [*sic*] Dávila Francisco Arce Mariano Dols Benigno Cardozo, aide-de-camp Lorenzo Vera, assistant	**Bolivians from Tarija:** Baldomero Vera Bernardino Valverdi Julián Romero Jacinto Gaite
Bolivians from Caiza:	**Bolivians from Caiza:** Nemecio Valverdi Miguel Montero Estanislao Zeballos Francisco Zeballos	**Bolivians from Caiza:** Nemecio Valverdi Miguel Montero Estanislao Zeballos Francisco Zeballos

The discrepancies between the two texts stem first of all from their date of publication. On March 23, *El Trabajo* published the list of those who left Tarija for the San Francisco mission, but not all intended to participate in the expedition proper: this was the case of Demócrito Cabezas, a prefectural delegate, of his secretary, Tomás Molina, and of his aide-de-camp, Benigno Cardozo. Likewise once they arrived at the Pilcomayo, four Criollos, from Yacuiba and Caiza, signed on; naturally these do not feature on the list first published by the Tarija newspaper. Benardo Trigo added them to his own list at a later time.

On the other hand, the list of May 11 is that of the actual expedition members. Even if we eliminate Demócrito Cabezas and his aides, the list still differs from that of March: this could explain Ringel's deserter story. In effect it seems probable that the "surplus" names on the March list, which do not figure on that drawn up in May, are precisely those of persons who decided not to leave with Crevaux. In this hypothesis, the number of seventeen travelers indicated by Crevaux seems the more plausible. I would add that, among the Bolivians from Tarija, Baldomero Vera is indicated as leader of the Bolivian delegation, with "secret instructions" for the expedition's arrival at Asunción: it seems that, in the event of success, the Bolivian government did not want the credit to go to Crevaux alone.[10]

But there remain unknowns concerning both the Indian and the French explorers. Although most contemporary sources speak of the interpreter, Iramaye, in his letters of April 17, Crevaux gives another name: Chiriqui. Since the same documents talk about a single interpreter, we might think they are the same person, for instance that Chiriqui was the nickname of Iramaye … were it not for an isolated indication provided by Thouar in 1884, which mentions *two* interpreters.[11] A mystery I have not been able to elucidate.

The other doubt concerns the French victims. In his biographical dictionary, the Argentinian, Vicente Cutolo, records a disconcerting piece of information: he reports that, along with Crevaux, the artist André Laustau, "who always accompanied him,"[12] also died. The problem is that no such person exists, at least not in our story. Checking all of the biographies of Crevaux, I find no Laustau who accompanied him on his expeditions and, in fact, all of the Frenchmen on the 1882 expedition were traveling with him for the first time; as for the expedition artist, he is identified as Auguste Ringel, an Alsatian. I have been unable to discover the source of this confusion, which was repeated word for word by

Josep Barnadas in his article "Crevaux, Julio" in the *Diccionario Histórico de Bolivia*.[13]

Whatever the case, Cutolo's erroneous information remains an isolated incident. The lists of French explorers pose a different problem. For once, all of the contemporary documents concur, and all of the later texts report the presence of five Frenchmen: but their names do not coincide. Either the French and Bolivian sources diverge or, like the texts of Thouar and Novis, they are written by people having been in Bolivia.

In 1884 in France, one of Crevaux's first biographers lists the French victims of the expedition: "An already distinguished astronomer, Me. [*sic*, Louis] Billet; an artist, Jules [*sic*, Auguste] Ringel; a licensed naval helmsman, E. Haurat; and an aide-de-camp, J. Didelot,"[14] as well as, naturally, Crevaux himself. The same list (minus the errors in first names) features, for instance in Broc's dictionary, and even on French Internet sites such as "Les Amis de Jules Crevaux,"[15] which also proposes a photo of the five explorers taken before they left France.

The Bolivian sources and those of the travelers present in Bolivia at the time diverge on one name in this list: they substitute Didelot for Dumigron. This time the confusion has an explanation. Joseph Didelot's name was actually Jean-François Payeur. Born in Paris of parents from Alsace-Lorraine, he lived in the Lorraine village of Lorquin, Crevaux's hometown, and soon became his secretary. At the time, Lorraine was still part of the German Empire, having been annexed after the 1870 war, and the young man changed his name in order to avoid the Prussian military service. In 1881, at just seventeen years of age, he accompanied Crevaux to Buenos Aires with the intention of following him on his fourth expedition.[16]

However, Crevaux himself asked Didelot to give up the idea of going farther because of his young age: indeed on January 4, Crevaux wrote a note conveying this and recommending the young man to the French consul in Buenos Aires.[17] The young man from Lorraine thus never accompanied the expedition on the Pilcomayo, and in effect, in its issue dated July 14, 1882, the *Courrier de la Moselle* announced: "The Didelot boy, whom the newspapers announced as having died along with Doctor Crevaux, landed at Bordeaux on the 6th of this month, coming from Buenos Ayres [*sic*]; his arrival is awaited here from one moment to the next."[18] In the years that followed, Didelot became an explorer in his own right, but on the African continent, and in 1899, he published a book under the name of Payeur-Didelot. On the cover, apparently for marketing purposes, he presents himself as a "Former member of Dr. Crevaux's mission in the Gran Chaco." In addition, in his preface, Joseph-Victor Barbier writes that the author "was involved in the resounding catastrophe that engulfed the Crevaux mission: Mr. Payeur-Didelot is none other than the young Didelot, the explorer's secretary and sole survivor of the massacre of the mission led by the Lorraine explorer."[19]

Payeur-Didelot "survived" because he never set foot on the banks of the Pilcomayo. Nevertheless, for the French, his name continues to be listed among the victims, while the presence (and death) of another Frenchman, Jean Dumigron, is completely ignored. This figure, who lived at Sucre, joined the Crevaux expedition at Tupiza, on the Bolivian–Argentinian border. Thouar tells the story:

> Out of Mr. Aniceto Arce's house came Dumigron, a Frenchman who joined the Crevaux mission, the unfortunate fate of which he shared. He had scraped together a nest egg after working ten years as a horticulturalist. Still young—he was only thirty-two—he was returning to France to enjoy his savings; at Tupiza, he met Doctor Crevaux.
> —And where are you going? he asked him.
> —To Paris, via Tucuman and Buenos Aires.
> —Well, that's not the cheapest route. Come with us; we are going via the Pilcomayo; the trip will cost you nothing.

Enchanted, caught up, he left ... The rest is known![20]

Where did Crevaux die? The documents do not agree on this point either, and the place of the crime can be situated somewhere along a stretch of several tens of kilometers of the Pilcomayo, between Teyu upstream to Piquirenda downstream, or even lower. The uncertainty can stem from several factors: for instance, different toponyms in different languages for the same place. The real meaning of each toponym or the actual area it designates also give rise to confusion. The designations of Teyu or Cabayurepoti do not always indicate a precise spot on the map or a specific village. Rather they refer to zones at a certain level of the river, which include both banks. For example, the Tobas' Teyu, referring to a camp, may be located on the left bank of the Pilcomayo, but the opposite bank is also called Teyu along several kilometers. Upstream from the Tobas' Teyu and on the right bank, for example, there was the Criollo Santa Bárbara de Teyu, later known as the Crevaux Settlement. An editorial in the Tarija newspaper suggests another factor: the Indians did not want to indicate the exact spot for fear of appearing to be guilty

Figure 25. Teyu
Teófilo Novis, *El Chaco en imágenes* ([1887] 2016), p. 133.

or exposing themselves to revenge on the part of other groups: "This is the only explanation we can find for the fact that we still do not know where the barbaric murder took place."[21]

A first group of documents speaks of "Teyu." That is the case, for example, of Eudogio Raña's report of May 6, which he based on the testimony of Yahuanahua, or of the first announcement of the murder in the Tarija newspaper *El Trabajo* dated May 11, 1882. Francisco Arraya's telegram from the end of May also indicates "Tello" as the place of the crime. Paz Guillén, and Thouar in a later piece, are a little more specific, stating that the explorers were killed on the left bank of the river.[22] Now we know that the Toba groups living along this section of the Pilcomayo preferred this bank. And even if Francisco Zeballos does not make Teyu the scene of the crime, he, too, indicates that it took place on the left bank.

A year after the events, members of the Campos expedition provide different information. According to their version, the killing took place somewhere between Teyu, upstream, and Cabayurepoti, downstream. As he leaves the Crevaux Settlement (formerly Santa Bárbara de Teyu) downstream, Thouar says: "We are passing through the place where the Crevaux mission was massacred." At the same spot, and therefore before reaching Cabayurepoti, Campos confirms: "We are in the Teyu zone, we are across from the place where Crevaux and his companions were sacrificed." And Paz Guillén himself, who earlier mentioned only a vague "Teyu," notes that between the Crevaux Settlement and Cabayurepoti the expedition passes "specifically over the theater of the bloody murder of the scientist, Crevaux."[23]

It is possible that this precise spot is that mentioned in a letter from the *El Trabajo* correspondent known as Nido del Cuervo ("Crow's Nest"), which lies between Teyu and Caballero-ipoti [*sic*].[24] But again, and because of its location, this place may correspond to another toponym appearing in the documents: on March 10, 1883, an anonymous letter from Caiza addressed to the senator Bernardo Trigo reports that Crevaux died "in a place that the savages call Cuvarocai," more specifically on the right bank of the river.[25] Natalio Roldán, on the other hand, citing information given him by the members of the 1883 Ibaceta expedition, talks about "Curavocai," and adds that this is a place five leagues downstream from "Tello or Tellú." This toponym does not come from the Guarani, but more likely from the Toba language; it is also possible that *Cuvaro* is the Indian pronunciation of the Spanish *cuervo* (just as, for instance, the Chiriguano call the "cross"—*cruz* in Spanish—*curusu*).

But another document gives Cabayurepoti as the place of the crime. In effect, that is where the Tobas are thought to have decided to kill the explorers, according to a letter dated June 8, written by a Franciscan. But clearly things are not that simple, and Thouar gives contradictory information. If, as we have just seen, he locates the crime site somewhere between Teyu and Cabayurepoti, a few pages earlier he says something different: there he writes that the travelers arrived safely at Cabayurepoti on April 25, left the next day, only to be murdered on the 27th on a beach downstream. This version has its defenders: the Franciscan Alejandro Corrado also maintains that Crevaux was killed "a few kilometers upstream from Piquirenda," in other words, downstream from Cabayurepoti.[26] More importantly, this version coincides with the firsthand testimony of Francisco Zeballos. The Franciscans even give a specific toponym in this case: Güiraitarenda. The annals of the Tarija convent mention this name in 1883, and two years later, Giannecchini again indicates it as the spot where Crevaux died, a short distance downstream from Cabayurepoti.[27] And yet in August 1882, according to the Gran Chaco subprefect, the Tobas at the San Francisco mission claimed the crime had taken place "downstream from Piquirenda."[28]

It is very hard to get a clear picture in the midst of such disparate information. The specific toponym indicated by the Franciscans, and the fact that the geographic location of Güiraitarenda corresponds to Zeballos's testimony might tip the scales in its favor; but the Criollos and the Argentinians are also precise in their information, and they indicate Cuvarocai and/or Nido del Cuervo, at any rate some place upstream. In all events, and even if several documents indicate that the killers were from there, it seems we can eliminate Teyu *stricto sensu*, and the most precise information indicates a place farther downriver. Those who give Teyu as the crime site seem to have used the toponym in a generic sense, and in particular because the spot was known as the Tobas' "capital." It follows then, that the military settlement that immortalized Crevaux's name a year later does not indicate the place of his death for posterity.

The versions in circulation of the circumstances of the killing are just as diverse and—no surprise—do not always coincide with each other. Curiously the least detailed is the version of Francisco Zeballos, a witness and survivor of the massacre, who says simply that "everyone disembarked ... While they were walking along, without a care, trustingly, and separated the ones from the others, the perfidious Tobas attacked them and carried out their barbaric, bloodthirsty plan."[29] The other versions usually stress three points: a preexisting plan to massacre the explorers (this is something that Zeballos, too, suggests); the treachery of the Indians, who were able to kill the travelers only by laying a trap for them; and Crevaux's foolhardiness.

As for the weapons used in the crime, these vary with the account: clubs, spears, knives, arrows, or all of the above. Francisco Zeballos speaks of clubs, and the correspondent of *El Trabajo* of sticks, which comes down to the same thing. Paz Guillén talks of explorers "pierced by arrows or battered with clubs." Thouar mentions clubs and knives and, in 1906, describes a Toba club, adding: "It was with this weapon that they bashed in the skulls of Doctor Crevaux and his companions." Roldán, for his part, claims that the murder was committed with clubs, knives, and spears.[30]

Eudogio Raña, however, informed by the Chiriguano, Yahuanahua, stresses that the Tobas stabbed the travelers to death with knives, and he links this *modus operandi* to the immediate cause of the killing. In his version, Crevaux and his companions had begun to hand out gifts among the Indians, which set off a riot and an attempt on the part of the Tobas to appropriate all of the travelers' belongings. He writes that they were killed with the very knives they had given out. But Raña goes on to say that the whole thing had been planned in advance:

The Tobas developed this plan with the Tapiétis [*sic*] and the Chiriguanos, as soon as the Toba woman taken from Tarija was freed and had told them everything they were carrying with them and why they were traveling on the river, which they wanted to explore to open a way to the Paraguay; and that was something they detested wholeheartedly because they knew full well that their lands, their wild freedom, and their trade as thieves would be taken from them.[31]

The Indian from Itiyuru, who brought the news of the explorers' murder, clearly confirmed as much later, saying that he had seen nothing but he knew for sure from the Indians that it was true that, once the Toba girl taken from Tarija was set free at the San Francisco mission, the Tapiétis [*sic*], Tobas, and Chiriguanos resolved to betray them.[32]

The Toba girl taken from Tarija was, of course, Yallá. Without mentioning the girl, other authors also write of the gifts handed out and evoke betrayal by the Tobas:

Crevaux began to hand out gifts. The Indians themselves helped the explorers to take them out of their boats to distribute them. Suddenly one of the leaders, who seemed to be the paramount chief, said to his soldiers in his language: "Rather than take these gifts little by little, it would be better to take them once and for all by killing these foreigners." And immediately he blew the horn that he wore around his neck, and a crowd of Toba Indians appeared as though by magic from the surrounding woods. Shortly afterwards, Doctor Crevaux and his companions were massacred.[33]

Leocadio Trigo no doubt used this same version as a basis several years later.

Mr. Creveaux [*sic*] no doubt gave the Tobas gifts and wanted to take a photo of himself standing in front of the many savages and sharing out valuables. He prepared the camera, and, when the photo was about to be taken, they gave the signal for the killing, without anyone having noticed the least sign of this horrific plan.[34]

It may be that the incident of the camera later served as a pretext for the scam mounted by Roger de Courteville, which I mentioned earlier. In all events, in evoking a crowd of Tobas just waiting or "this horrible plan," the author of the letter written in 1883 and Leocadio Trigo agree with Raña in affirming that the massacre was prepared in advance.

Other versions make no mention of the gifts distributed by Crevaux: the Indians (and Cuserai in the first place) are reported to have simply lured the travelers to disembark by inviting them to a meal of mutton and fish, the better to kill them afterward.[35] Whatever the case, this was also a planned betrayal, the result of the "palaver" held a few days earlier to decide to kill the travelers.

Others maintain that the Tobas simply seized the opportunity offered by the circumstances. According to Luis Paz, Crevaux had come to a point where navigation was no longer possible because the river was too low. The Tobas were reported to have said that the Paraguay was barely four days' travel away and they would help transport his things: "Doctor Crevaux accepted their offer, and they disembarked to continue on foot, fully trusting the savages whose numbers were growing by the minute. At a given moment, more than twenty savages seized the explorers and clubbed them to death."[36] According to Roldán, the poor quality of the boats worked in favor of the killing:

> The boats that the unfortunate French explorer had had built at the San Francisco mission were no more than simple boxes, without curves or solidity, with a square stern and no tiller, with no oarlocks for using the oars with precision, and the members of the crew were seated in precarious positions. They endeavored to make frequent landings, which in my opinion allowed the Tobas, who were watching, to surprise and deceive them.[37]

In truth, this explanation is an isolated occurrence, and it is doubtful that a veteran of river exploration like Crevaux and an expert helmsman like Haurat would have decided to travel in boats so ill-suited to navigation. But the important point is that here, too, the question of deceit and betrayal crops up.

I found only two references to any armed resistance on the part of the explorers, or at least indicating that they were armed. In June 1882, the *El Trabajo* correspondent announces: "A Noten [an Indian group] recently arrived from the Pilcomayo reported that two members of the crew fought until they were exhausted, and the savages killed them only with great difficulty, when their ammunition gave out."[38] Much later, the Anglican missionary, W. Barbrooke Grubb, writes that, according to the natives' accounts collected in the Paraguayan Chaco, the killing happened because one of the explorers disobeyed Crevaux and opened fire on a Toba.[39] This is the only version I know of which does not make the Indians directly responsible for the crime.

Yet according to many other authors, the explorers did not defend themselves because they were not armed, and that, too, was the consequence of a trap. These versions relate that the travelers were unarmed in response to the desires expressed by the perfidious Tobas: "As they were disembarking, the Tobas came up to them and said: 'do not bring out your weapons; we don't have any, so why get them out? If you are not hostile, we won't be either.'"[40] And that is supposedly how the Tobas killed the travelers without their firing a single shot.

From there to blaming Crevaux was a short step that many did not hesitate to take. Luis Paz cannot understand how Crevaux could have been so trusting and laid down his weapons: "What blind credulity!"[41] According to Francisco Zeballos:

> They spent the 21st within sight of Bella Esperanza, a host of Indians greeted them, and they in turn made them gifts. When the Indians left, they, satisfied with the gifts, and Crevaux, with the peace achieved, he had a shot fired in the air, *promising them that they would now never make use of their weapons.* Crevaux immediately gathered up the ammunition from all of the members [of the expedition], saying that they needed to use it sparingly and that the bullets were not necessary because the Indians were calm; that they needed to avoid any shooting so that the Indians would not doubt the peace and friendship he had promised them, and that this is how he had already succeeded on other expeditions ... The ban on weapons went as far as not allowing [the men] to carry knives when going ashore so as not to frighten the Indians, so that, on the day of the killing *no one fired for lack of ammunition*, whereas they would have had time to defend themselves.42

This made for an easy killing, without pity, without the victims defending themselves. It also made for a polemic, because it is hard to understand how a seasoned traveler like Crevaux could have let himself be so easily deceived by the Indians. Indeed many frontier settlers questioned the excessive and imprudent lack of caution on the part of Crevaux, who had ignored all advice and warnings. According to Eudogio Raña, the people of Caiza had explained to the explorer that the Tobas were dangerous, but he had not listened. The subprefect concludes: "Mr. Crevaux's whims, haste, and overconfidence in peace and the gifts distributed to the Tobas caused his death and that of the rest, whereas myself, like many others, had informed him of the treacherous nature of the Toba savages."[43] Other Criollos belabored the point: "The explorer unwisely believed the Indians' word," "his overconfidence prompted the loss of the intrepid traveler," "Mr. Crevaux's trust in the Indians prompted the loss of the whole crew and of himself."[44] Others, who were not settlers, shared this opinion. According to the Argentinian Baldrich, even if the Pilcomayo was dangerous, "the river was certainly not a factor in the painful failure of this attempt, but rather the extreme confidence of its leader, who relied on the Toba Indians' treacherous loyalty";[45] for Wagner, a short time later, "Crevaux had been extremely imprudent" in going ashore unarmed.[46]

Distancing themselves from these harsh reprimands, other authors prefer to think that Crevaux and his companions succumbed under the number of their assailants, and mention the unlikely figure of "more than a thousand," and even nearly two thousand Indians.[47]

The explorers' deaths were merely the prelude to other, even more gruesome scenes. The horror, the morbid imagination, and the sensationalism of some, and the interest of others in stressing the Indians' cruelty the better to punish them all contributed to paint the victims' *postmortem* fate in the darkest colors.

After having killed them, Thouar claims, the Indians cut up the explorers' bodies and carried them off like war booty. In such conditions, how could one hope to recover the victims' remains? Indeed, the Frenchman Milhomme, from Carapari, is dubious and writes nearly a year after the crime:

> There has been much talk of searching for the remains of the Crevaux mission. I venture to point out that this goal seems to me rather difficult to achieve. The Tobas do not bury their enemies, and all the less when these are whitemen. The bones, once stripped of their flesh, are disputed by the women. The skull goes to a warrior ... this is the worthiest trophy for him. The top is sawed off to make a cup for drinking *aleka*. The women take the vertebrae, through which they pass a string; they make these into a belt, whose rattling accompanies their songs and dances.[48]

Milhomme is not the only one to think this way. Paz Guillén, too, imagines that the Tobas may have kept the cadavers in order to drink chicha from the skulls, which, according to Baldridge, was an ingrained tradition with them: "They drink *aloja*, but the cup that contains the repulsive liquid is not always an earthen vessel or a gourd. They often replace these with a human skull, which is handed around, brimming with yellowish liqueur."[49]

How much can we credit these macabre descriptions? That the remains of enemies killed in fighting were used as vessels in drinking feasts is a fact among Chaco Indians like the Tobas, the Nivaclés, the Chorotes, etc. Nevertheless, in the immense majority of cases, it was not the skull that was used but the scalp. This is not the appropriate place for what would necessarily be an incomplete description or analysis of the symbolic, ritual, and social value of human trophies among Indigenous Chaco warrior societies. It is enough to mention that the feasts of fermented drink following a war were usually held a month or more after the victory, depending on the time needed to prepare the scalp—which was dried, smoked, and sewn together on two sides at the forehead and the neck to form a receptacle. Depending on the place, this practice endured until the Chaco War in the 1930s.[50] Even if the skull itself could sometimes be used as a drinking cup, it was not the general practice, and it was usually discarded once the scalp had been removed. More important for us, according to the different authors, the scalps and/or skull of whitemen were less valued than those of other Indians, and some even claim that the Tobas did not scalp white people. And even if the taking of this hair was the occasion for numerous rites and drinking feasts, there is no reference to monthly celebrations of the full moon in which these scalps (or skulls) might be used, as Arancibia suggests in his report on "Crevaux's skull."

While this information does not allow us to deny them categorically, it does allow us to seriously doubt the claims advanced by Milhomme or Baldrich. Better still, if the Tobas really used Crevaux's skull to drink chicha, they apparently discarded the precious vessel, since, as we have seen, the skull was later found in the vicinity of Yanduñanca, near Teyu, and piously taken to Tarija.

Notwithstanding, José Correa warns that this skull did not belong to any of the travelers.

José Correa asserts that the skull found on the other bank does not belong to any of the Gringos, that it is no doubt that of a Noten or a Toba who died in the fight on November 6, 1887, at Santa Bárbara de Teyu; he says that the Tobas, with whom he was, had gone downriver to fish and saw some crows; upon drawing closer, they found the corpses in the water and transported them to the other bank so that the fish they were going to eat would not feed on human flesh ... Felizardo is not telling the truth when he says that they had taken Crevaux's head as a trophy and had celebrated for eight days. I'm warning you so that you do not take the skull of the Mataco for that of Crevaux. The Matacos must be very pleased to see that one of their skulls has been taken to Tarija (even in the belief that it was Crevaux's) and that it was given a splendid funeral.[51]

The authors diverge deeply on the victims' *postmortem* fate. While some collect "Crevaux's skulls," others tell it differently: the killers left the bodies on the bank ... with the exception, naturally, of Crevaux's, reserved for a special rite. No one is interested in the fact that the explorer perished with some fifteen companions: for those chronicling the crime, only Crevaux's remains are worthy of mention, and they attribute to the Tobas the same keen sense of preeminence. In respecting the hierarchy, the Indians seem, in these versions, to be the first to forge the "Crevaux myth."

Thus according to the letter addressed to the senator, Bernardo Trigo, written from Caiza on March 10, 1883, the corpses of the expedition members were abandoned on the beach, but "the Tobas carried that of Doctor Crevaux to a neighboring village with great ceremony. There they spent the night and until noon the next day singing around the body; then they buried it in a visible spot, not far from the huts."[52] Based on what the members of the Ibaceta expedition told him, Natalio Roldán recounts much the same thing:

All of the corpses, stripped and strangled, were placed in two of the boats. Carried away by the current, the boats sank in rapids some seven leagues from this place, and that is why our friend Fontana was unable to find the corpses of these martyrs when he traveled up the Pilcomayo. I know that, out of consideration, that of Crevaux was taken away by four leaders and buried near the place where they would eat mutton after having celebrated all night by dancing around the body.[53]

Roldán explains neither why the Tobas needed to strangle the already dead bodies nor how he "knew" that was how things had happened. In all events, he adds, it is all but impossible to locate Crevaux's remains:

"the place where he is buried is flooded every year by the river in spate, which washes away the topsoil and erases all landmarks."

As we have seen, José Correa does not agree with this version. For him, Crevaux and his men were murdered on the beach and the bodies left there, "with no one's head being cut off," and "the first flood carried them away." Abandoning his earlier version about bodies being chopped up and carried off as war prizes, Thouar adopts Correa's story in a later, fictionalized text: the victims were stripped naked and left on the bank for the vultures until the current swept them downstream.[54]

Without wandering skulls or honorific burial, this version is less sensationalist and has every chance of being right. But that does not make it any more acceptable, and, to date, rumors persist about another appalling fate having been visited on the victims' bodies: cannibalism. This theme could not fail to crop up when it came to wild, unsubjugated Indians. For Cutolo, "it is assumed that Crevaux, like several of his companions, was devoured by cannibals"; Numa Broc writes: "Crevaux and his companions were attacked, massacred, and probably devoured by the Tobas."[55] Corinne Fenchelle-Charlot calls the Tobas, Noctenes, and others "cannibals," and the back cover of her book indicates that Crevaux "died tragically, murdered and then eaten by the Toba Indians."[56] Francis Grandhomme, on the other hand, is more cautious, speaking of "the sinister reputation" of the Tobas, who are reputed to be "among the last cannibals on the planet"; and he cites a recent episode: at the "Fête de la Science 2005," the French Centre National de la Recherche Scientifique stand, represented chiefly by a professor from Paris X-Nanterre University, gave a glimpse of his search in Guyana for, in his own words, the school children "who would discover the story of Jules Crevaux, the French explorer eaten by the Indigenous cannibals he was studying."[57]

This legend seems to stem from Thouar's first account, that of the bodies dismembered by the Tobas. Imagination has done the rest. In reality, the cannibalistic Tobas exist only in the French texts or, like that by Cutolo, those written by outsiders. No one in Bolivia mentions cannibalism, and for good reason: the Tobas are not and have never been cannibals, which the above authors could have learned had they taken the trouble to consult any handbook of Chaco ethnology.

Allow me to recall here the episode reported by José Correa: "when they came closer, they found the corpses in the water and transported them to the other bank *so that the fish they were going to eat would not feed on human flesh.*" This story was well known to the frontier Criollos, who would not have failed to include this epithet among the other frightful adjectives that described the Tobas for them: bloodthirsty, perfidious, cruel, barbaric, or treacherous. But Crevaux had come away without a scratch from these earlier encounters with the Huitotos and other cannibals of Amazonia, and those who ultimately killed him on the banks of the Pilcomayo could have been no less cruel or savage. In the fevered European imagination, Thouar's dismembered trophies had turned into a banquet of human flesh.

CHAPTER 6

Beyond the Massacre

Although he presents himself as a former member of the Crevaux mission to the Chaco, Jean-François Payeur, alias Didelot, cannot be considered to be a "survivor" of a massacre from which he was absent. But immediately after the crime, rumors about other survivors of the Crevaux expedition began to circulate. In our current state of knowledge, it will surprise no one, then, that this information is more than confused or contradictory.

One certainty amid all the confusion, though. All authors agree on the existence of at least two survivors: Francisco Zeballos and the Chiriguano interpreter, Iramaye, from the Tigüipa mission.

The many Indians who arrived at the missions and Criollo villages after the murder quickly reported the news: "There are many Tobas and Notens in this mission, come from downstream … The Toba girl you brought back came as well, and she confirmed the explorers' death, with the exception of one very young man and the Chiriguano who left from San Francisco mission; it is believed that the surviving Christian is the son of Maître Ceballos."[1]

In the days that followed, the rumors multiplied: "Only two young men survived, one from Caiza and the other a neophyte from the Tigüipa mission, they have been taken captive, we don't know anything more"; "Francisco Cevallos [sic], a child of 12 or 15, son of the carpenter Francisco [sic, Estanislao] Cevallos, who was a member of the crew, and the Indian Yramaye [sic], the interpreter that Doctor Crevaux took along, are still alive, in the hands of the savages."[2] According to the Tarija papers, Francisco and Iramaye stayed behind to watch the boats when Crevaux and his men went ashore on April 27, and therefore escaped death.[3] Lastly, the news of their survival was confirmed by the Tobas who arrived at the San Francisco mission and offered to free them.

But the unanimity stops there. The Franciscan sources (much better informed in this case, since Francisco was set free thanks to the missionaries' mediation) and the subprefect Raña affirm that the young man arrived at the San Francisco mission on July 1. Despite this certainty, other authors do not hesitate to speak of a much longer captivity. In his 1884 text, Thouar says that the young Zeballos remained a prisoner for six months, information faithfully repeated by more recent authors.[4] Yet in May 1883, the same Thouar claims that Zeballos was freed on August 1, making a total of three months of captivity; in 1906 he repeats the same dates in his *Journal des Voyages*.[5]

The confusion is even greater when it comes to Francisco Zeballos himself. We know that he is the son of Estanislao Zeballos from Yacuiba, who joined the Crevaux mission at Caiza. But that does not prevent several authors from identifying Francisco as a young Indian from the Franciscan missions, "a little missionary Indian,"[6] probably confusing him with Iramaye. Others still, confusing the savior and the saved, make him a Catholic priest, and, for the Argentinian Geographical Institute, he is the "missionary Ceballos"; it is this information that arrives in France, where it is taken up, for example, by Jules Gors in an article on Crevaux's death.[7] At the root of this confusion was probably the expression "*Indio misionero*," literally "missionary Indian," but where *misionero* means "living at the mission, a neophyte," and not a friar at the mission whose calling is to convert. Finally yet other, less informed, authors, did not fail to make Francisco "the son of Doctor Zeballos," that is, of the director of the Buenos Aires Geographical Institute![8]

In the case of Iramaye, the versions diverge not on his identity but on the circumstances of his survival. Wounded in the attack of April 27, he is reported to have been captured by the Tobas. It is not clear whether Iramaye was effectively liberated at the same time as Zeballos or if he managed to escape. According to several authors, the Tobas "made prisoner the Indian interpreter that Crevaux had taken with him, a Chiriguano Indian called Iramayo [*sic*], from the Tigüipa mission, and he escaped after a few days";[9] "he crossed the desert after having been captured by the Tobas on the day of the massacre, and today is in

Ñancaroinza."[10] Yet as we have seen, according to Fr. Marcelleti, Iramaye remained with the Tobas of his own free will.

If the information on the sole survivors acknowledged by everyone is confused, we can imagine even more confusion when it comes to the others. All in all, the different documents mention four or five more survivors, but without agreeing on their identity and even less on their fate.

It is not clear if Iramaye is the same person as the expedition's cook, who, according to several authors, also managed to escape the massacre. The letter written by a Franciscan on June 8 affirms that the Tobas captured Zeballos, and "the cook who prepared the explorers' meals met the same fate." Later Wagner gives the same information, more or less: he reports that a sailor and the cook stayed on the boats, thus escaping the massacre,[11] which fits the versions that affirm that Iramaye and Francisco Zeballos did not go ashore. None of the documents gives the cook's name. He could therefore be Iramaye (doubling as interpreter and scullion), or the Chiriqui mentioned by Crevaux, if the name really designates someone other than Iramaye. In all events, the very fact of not having a name in the written documents suggests that the cook was not a whiteman but actually an Indian.

In his testimony of July 1882, Francisco Zeballos not only mentions Iramaye, he also reports the existence of other survivors:

> Zeballos indicates that the sailor N. Blanco, an Argentinian, is held captive at Teyu; and that Mr. Ernesto N. and Romero Rodríguez, at the time of Crevaux's murder, managed to escape into the forest to the south, in the direction of Itiyuru; and that several Tobas followed them for a long time, but lost their trail and abandoned the search. He also indicates that the interpreter Iramaye from the Tigüipa mission escaped with his life because he headed northward.[12]

> He saw Ernesto and Rodríguez escape, and he knows nothing about the others, not even his father. Upon returning to the San Francisco mission, by way of Teyu, he says he saw Blanco, who was barely able to tell him that he begged the Father and the Christians to save him. He adds that, during the two months of his captivity, he saw the Tobas wearing the clothes of all the explorers except those of the fugitives and of Blanco.[13]

Yet when talking with the missionaries at the San Francisco mission in August, the Tobas denied that Blanco was being held captive at Teyu and maintained that he had died along with the others—which, despite the Tobas' protests, was practically tantamount to admitting they were guilty of the crime.

Carmelo Blanco was one of the two Argentinian sailors who accompanied the Crevaux mission on orders from their government. Thouar calls him "Chilata," and notes this important detail: "According a letter just sent me by Mr. Lacombe, the chief mechanic on the Argentinian battleship, *El Plata*, Chilata was a Toba and had served four years as a deckhand."[14] Chilata was probably captured as a child on the "frontier" of the Argentinian Chaco. Whatever the case, whether or not they recognized him as one of their own, the Tobas on the upper Pilcomayo did not afford him a better fate.

The other survivor mentioned, Ernesto, is Ernest Haurat, the French naval helmsman. On the other hand, it is harder to identify Romero, or "Romero Rodríguez," or Romero and Rodríguez. In fact, the only Rodríguez we find on the list of expedition members is Enrique, the other Argentinian sailor and a colleague of Blanco; the only Romero is Julián Romero, from Tarija. To further complicate matters, the Tarija prefect makes Romero and Rodríguez two Bolivian citizens, and Thouar also speaks of Rodríguez as being Bolivian.[15] Furthermore Eudogio Raña does little to clarify matters when, instead of Romero, he mentions that a "Moreno" survived together with "the little Frenchman Ernesto."[16]

Even more confusing: after the initial news reports, no one talks about Rodríguez, and I found only one reference that still mentions Romero, in October 1882: the subprefect of Salinas Province, Elías Vacaflor, acknowledges receipt of one hundred pesos sent by the prefecture and "meant to aid the unfortunate Julián Romero and Hernesto Aurat [*sic*], survivors of the fatal Crevaux mission."[17] After this mention, Romero, too, disappears from the documentation.

Having gotten this far, we could list the survivors of the massacre as follows:

1. Francisco Zeballos
2. Iramaye
3. The cook? If indeed this was not Iramaye. In all events, he is not mentioned further.
4. Ernest Haurat
5. Carmelo Blanco
6. Enrique Rodríguez
7. Julián Romero

But naturally not everyone is in agreement. Another key witness, José Correa, contradicts these reports: "According to José, who witnessed the events, they left only young Zevallos [*sic*] alive, and all the others died at the same time and in the same place."[18] A few months later, Correa contradicts himself once again and this time claims that two men managed to escape downstream in a boat, only to be captured later by the Noctenes or the Matacos living on the right bank of the river.[19]

Later reports mention only Blanco and Haurat among the captured survivors. It is to them that Milhomme is referring in his letter about two prisoners the Chiriguano were reported to have seen among the Tobas, a letter that arrived in France and prompted Thouar's trip in 1883. As for the fate of these two survivors, the information is as varied as it is unsure, and even in part verges on the fantastic.

For Thouar (with whom Novis agrees on this point), Blanco was not captured immediately but escaped with Haurat: he thus assigns him the role played by Rodríguez in Zeballos's version. In this story, Blanco and Haurat are reported to have fled along the right bank of the Pilcomayo (the crime having taken place on the opposite side) in an attempt to reach Itiyuru to the west, but were captured almost immediately.[20]

The expedition led by Campos in 1883 yields some frightful news. Although he quotes José Correa's letter, which denies the existence of any survivors, Paz Guillén writes this note, in which the young Yallá appears once more:

> Among the martyrs, the French helmsman Haurat and an Argentinian, Carmelo Blanco, also escaped and were taken prisoner and saved thanks to the tender influence and charity of the Indian woman, Yallá, who prevented their death. They bore their captivity for five months, at the end of which they died, sacrificed perhaps … Perhaps they were immolated at one of their festivals, putting them to a slow death and dancing around them to increase the pains of their agony![21]

Thouar, too, gathered similar information and sent it to the Société de Géographie de Paris: while he was at the Crevaux Settlement, he reports, the Tobas told him that the prisoners "were seen for the last time tied to trees and serving as targets on whom children and women practiced their skill."[22] This means that, even though he does not mention it in his 1884 text, Thouar was already familiar with this version of Haurat and Blanco's suffering, which he describes in detail in his 1891 book:

they "perished after suffering most atrociously, bound to the trunks of *algarrobos* [carob trees] and being used as targets for the Indians' arrows. This ordeal went on for nearly six months."[23] Novis in turn describes the captives' painful end:

> They died suffering cruelly: tied to thick tree trunks, they were used as targets for the arrows of Toba youths; the entertainment consisted (a barbaric refinement) in not hitting them but surrounding them with arrows fired into the trunk to which they were tied; naturally some were clumsy and struck the bodies of the unfortunate men. This ordeal went on for nearly six months; oblivion was the martyrs' only reward.[24]

As "barbaric" as the Tobas may have been, such an ordeal, of such duration, seems rather unlikely and in any case admits of a certain amount of doubt. According to Baldrich, among the Tobas, "Christian prisoners are destined to become the slaves of headmen, who exhaust them through hard labor, hardship, and ill-treatment ... They are often exchanged or returned by the Bolivian missionaries on the upper Pilcomayo, but at other times they are brutally killed during the tribe's big celebrations and drunken revelries."[25] Thouar, on the contrary but in a late text, writes that the Tobas never kill their white prisoners, which adds a touch of mystery to the fate of Haurat and Blanco:

> Never do the Indians, not even the most savage ones, strike a Whiteman who comes to them alone, unarmed, unless they are driven to do so by drink ... In all other circumstances, they are incapable of such cowardly behavior and, aware of their strength, will respect the prisoner with the cold indifference that his weakness inspires in them ... Between 1862 and 1884, of the eleven Bolivian prisoners, men, women, children, taken by the Tobas following hostilities that could cause retaliation, all, without distinction, were given their freedom after a longer or shorter period of captivity.[26]

Thouar cites the example of José Correa, who "was present when Crevaux was massacred" and was freed after nearly twenty years of captivity. And he concludes: "The murder of Haurat and Blanco, after Zeballos was freed, are, in this Bolivian border zone, a unique exception, an unprecedented occurrence!" It may be that Thouar wants, once again, to suggest the secret participation of the missionaries in the massacre of the Crevaux mission and its survivors.

Another unknown is the identity of the Indians who finished off Haurat and Chilata. Indeed, if most authors point to the Tobas, other versions exist: in the 1884 issue of the journal *Science*, the two survivors appear as captives of the Chorotes—and this information comes from Thouar himself.[27] José Correa, who first says there were no survivors, later states they were captured by the Noctenes or the Matacos; this version is probably the origin of the fictionalized story published by Thouar in 1906, in which he relates that the prisoners were in the hands of the Mataguayos on the right bank of the Pilcomayo.

Beyond confused information and unlikely ordeals, the uncertain fate of the survivors stoked imaginations, and authors definitively crossed the fine line that might still separate history, however vague, from pure and simple fable.

The first, or one of the first, is Théophile Novis, in the novel he began in France and published years later in Bolivia. This book tells the story of a French hero (Novis himself) initially a prisoner of the Matacos living on the Bermejo River in Argentina and then of the Tobas on the Bolivian side of the Pilcomayo. The characters, the settings, and the events of the novel are drawn from the experience Novis acquired on the expedition led by Thouar in 1887. For instance, when he was among the Matacos, a girl fell in love with the hero: her name is Yala, and we recognize the Toba girl, Yallá, whom we have already met, and whom Novis, too, had met. Then, when he was with the Tobas, the hero fell in love with and married a young woman of mixed blood, Ita. Ita's mother was a Toba. As for her father, she is made to say:

> I didn't know my father, but I know he was a man of your race, who was a prisoner like you; but he was made to suffer greatly. My mother, who was young, cared for him, and when she had given birth to me, to punish her for having had relations with my father, he was tied to a tree for half of the day, and the children and young people would entertain themselves by outlining his body with arrows they shot into the tree trunk; as some of them were clumsy, every day he received three, four, ten arrows in his body, and it was only after six months of suffering that my father died in the arms of my mother, who loved him madly.[28]

And Ita's father would tell his Toba lover, in French, *Je t'aime, tu es bonne*. This story, no doubt possible, was that of Haurat.

Later Thouar, too, takes an interest in Haurat. Naturally his fate intrigues his fellow countryman more than the unlikely fate of a half-Toba like Blanco-Chilata. In 1906 in his *Journal des voyages*, Thouar publishes a long account which fully benefits from the authority he enjoyed as an explorer who set out in search of Crevaux's remains; in fact, it is another fictional account, a piece of mediocre literature, a tear-jerker even, which toward the end turns into a hymn to the unfortunate helmsman.

In this version, Haurat and Blanco escape and hide in the Cabayurepoti marshes, on the right bank of the river, thinking to make their way to Itiyuru to seek help. The fugitives are on the territory of the Mataguayo Indians; exhausted and famished, they intend to seek out the Indians because they had given the passing expedition a warm welcome. In this way, they come to a village, where the men tie them to a carob tree, but do not harm them, and feed them. Yet some ten days later, some Toba leaders come to the village and they discuss the prisoners with the Mataguayos:

> After the Tobas left, they were tied separately to trees; shortly before sunset, Blanco, Haurat's unfortunate companion, was taken southward to another *rancheria* belonging to the Mataguayos, while Haurat, whose legs had been bound for the first time, was taken back under heavy guard to the *rancho*. Now alone, Haurat understood that he was lost and expected to die the next day. But not at all. When the sun rose, he was tied to the same *algarrobo* trunk, but this time solidly attached; the Indians did not repel the children who came to practice their skills with bow and arrow, and neglected to give him drink and food.

But the hero cannot die so quickly:

> The sun's rays blaze down on your naked, emaciated body.
> The flies feed on your blood, dripping from your ever more numerous wounds.
> Thirst, horrible thirst, convulses your eyes, your tongue, your throat.
>   The "galinazos" [*sic*], vultures, come, slow their spiraling flight, descend, even brush you with their wings; the boldest prepare to carve up, starting with the eyes, then the anus, your miserable carcass which is not yet a corpse!

Figure 26. Haurat's ordeal
Arthur Thouar, "Sur les bords du Pilcomayo. Massacrés par les Tobas" (1906b), p. 76.

> … You bow your head: a final spasm, and your eyes stare forever
> in the fixity of death
> *Tumparens peguata chinureta.*
> Sleep in peace, poor little sailor![29]

If the French authors dwell on their compatriots' suffering, others give their imaginations freer rein. We could not have done without a version like that reported by Wagner in 1910: far from having succumbed to the arrows of the Indigenous children, the sailor actually escaped after his companions were massacred. "He swam down the Pilcomayo, feeding on fruit, roots, and fish; half-dead, he came to a place across from Asunción in Paraguay. He left an account of his miraculous descent down the Pilcomayo which still is a source of amazement for the people of Paraguay."[30]

Chilata-Blanco interests no one; the tragic fate of the French contingent attracts much more attention. Crevaux himself could not be forgotten, and he appears in another story associated with another famous explorer of the Pilcomayo: the Spaniard Enrique de Ibarreta, who, in 1898, set off downstream from the San Francisco mission, following the route of the 1882 French expedition. In a version reported by Bernardo Trigo, despite the sixteen years that had elapsed since April 27, 1882, Ibarreta is supposed to have stated that he "had been sent by a French society in search of the remains of the explorer Creveaux [*sic*]. He had documents from our legate in Paris which proved the truth of his claims ... He was going in search of Mr. Creveaux because he was reported to be the prisoner of a Toba tribe."[31]

Enrique de Ibarreta, too, disappeared on the Pilcomayo, farther downstream from Crevaux. When he came to the Patiño Falls, he was forced to stop because of navigational problems. He sent eight of his men on foot to Asunción; only two arrived. Nothing more was heard from the Spaniard. Was he dead? Or a prisoner of the Indians? As in the case of Crevaux, rumors ran rife, and this reflection in a Paraguayan paper would make a suitable epigraph: "The conjectures and reflections sparked by the contradictory telegrams and the thousands of pieces of information arriving from all over Bolivia and Argentina concerning the Ibarreta expedition are so numerous that the imagination becomes lost in an ocean of conjectures and yields the most fanciful hypotheses."[32]

Those who believe he died compare his death directly with that of Jules Crevaux: "After Crevaux, Ibarreta! ... He perished, like Crevaux, at the hands of the Orejudos, [who are] as cruel as the Tobas."[33] The Spaniard's death also prompted Thouar to again write, in 1899, about the Crevaux expedition and to accuse the Franciscans—and that was not the least of the ties linking the two explorers after death.

Although in 1899 the Bouchard expedition, sent on the trail of the Spaniard, concluded categorically that he had been killed by the "Orejudos" (Pilagas), not everyone accepted this verdict. Miguel Ortiz, a friend of Ibarreta's, writes in May 1899: "Might Ibarreta be the first civilized man who managed to share the life of the Chaco savages?"[34] And later still, Leocadio Trigo tells the following story:

> Mr. Ibarreta, of Herculean constitution, athlete extraordinaire, and possessed of a steely character as hard as the Toledo swords, stayed behind to live with the savages, who gave him a warm welcome. It was not long before he came to be seen as a higher being by the tribe that took him in. He enjoyed the status of a powerful sorcerer. His intelligence, his knowledge, and his physical vigor allowed him to

present himself as an extraordinary being, who worked miracles by predicting natural phenomena which seemed like veritable prophecies to the savages. The Indians tell that he married into the tribe and must have had children. He was admired by, but also beloved of, the savages. Supplied with ammunition and excellent weapons, he was a great hunter, and for that he sometimes traveled long distances from the village where he lived. One day, perhaps driven by hunger, he killed a domestic animal belonging to a distant tribe, who for this insignificant reason killed him. His death was intensely felt and mourned by the tribe with which he lived.[35]

Later yet Bernardo Trigo completed this account by signaling the existence of a communiqué purported to have been sent by the Spanish representative in Buenos Aires in June 1900: Ibarreta was still alive, and "married to the daughter of the headman, Sumallen."[36] And even though Trigo took pains to add that "nothing of all this has been proven," it made little difference. Through their deaths or their possible survival, the stories of Haurat, Crevaux, and Ibarreta merge and fuel the legend of the Pilcomayo, throwing an ever-thicker cloak of mystery over the fates of these men.

The legend of the survivors of the Crevaux expedition ends with an Anastasia syndrome *avant la lettre*: the appearance in 1886 of a certain Foyer or Fouaillet, who claimed to be one of the expedition members who had managed to escape from the Pilcomayo Indians. Under the title "a remnant of the Crevaux expedition," the Tarija papers reprint for the occasion an article from the Argentinian newspaper, *La Vos de la Iglesia*:

> Mr. Enrique Foyer, one of the members of the Crevaux expedition speared to death by the Toba Indians on the Pilcomayo, has arrived in the neighboring capital on the steamboat *Rivadavia*.
> Mr. Foyer says they were surprised by some forty Indians, who attacked them with spears, leaving them all without life.
> The explorer was fortunate to receive only two thrusts and lost consciousness from his wounds. When he came to, he saw his companions lying dead beside him, left there until the Indians returned to cut up the corpses as is their custom and to share them out as war trophies. Finding he was still alive, they captured him, bound up his wounds, and, after two years of living among these savages and eating nothing but maize and fish, three missionaries arrived and bought his freedom for ten liters of eau-de-vie.

Now free, with only a sheet for a garment, he came to an Argentinian province where he met a friend who gave him something to wear and a ticket for Buenos Aires, from whence he embarked for Montevideo.[37]

The French Foreign Affairs minister was obliged to apply to the Société de Géographie de Paris to confirm that no Fouaillet had even been a member of the Crevaux expedition and thus identify him as an imposter. Thouar, who, for his part, was in Sucre preparing a second expedition, also publicly denied Fouaillet's "fantastic account" and asked the Franciscans to testify in the same sense.[38] Apparently this person was a professional impostor who, using the names Louis Borea and Raoul Breton, had already been behind several scams in Chile and Argentina. [39]

Between the myths and the rumors, the only proven fact was the fate of Iramaye and Francisco Zeballos, the immediate survivors, who reappeared on the Chaco frontier. The destiny of their companions remains and will probably always remain a mystery.

We now need to answer two outstanding questions: Who were the guilty parties? And what was the motive for the crime?

CHAPTER 7

Faceless Killers

Crevaux and his crew were killed by Indians: that is a point on which, for once, documents and witnesses all agree; and we have no reason to doubt them. But from there on, the versions diverge considerably as to the identity of these Indians and their true role—absolutely guilty or simple material authors—which extends the range of suspects but also raises the question of motive: Who benefits from the crime?

The most frequently mentioned culprits are the Tobas. Examining the documents more closely, the accusation narrows at times (suspects' names are given), but at other times, the spectrum of possible killers broadens, as though all of the Indians in the Chaco were gathered on the banks of the Pilcomayo on April 27, 1882. And other culprits, more sinister because more dissimulated, appear: perfidious Franciscans, on the one hand, accused by the Criollo settlers with the later approval of Arthur Thouar; and merciless Criollos, on the other hand, who were said to have urged the Indians to take revenge on innocent victims.

Although nothing is really certain, evidence recovered in the months or years following the massacre could indicate several guilty parties among the Indians. Most of the indications point to the Tobas, beginning with Francisco Zeballos's testimony, in which he claims, in July 1882, that they hold the travelers' effects. Shortly after the crime, a Toba arrived at the San Francisco mission wearing Jean Dumigron's jacket. Likewise, the coins belonging to Crevaux or his box recovered in November 1882 were in the possession of the Tobas, and it was also the Tobas who later returned Crevaux's revolver to Giannecchini and Haurat's jersey to Thouar.

Nevertheless it is hard to consider these objects as compelling proof of guilt. People and things circulate, and they circulated a lot on the Pilcomayo during this period. For example, the coins recovered at the San Francisco mission were brought to the mission to exchange for food. In July 1882, questioned by Fr. Marcelleti, the Tobas Iñiri, Caligagae, and Cutaicoliqui also claimed that the Noctenes took the travelers' money to Itiyuru to be exchanged for cheese, dried meat, and other commodities. A short time later, Thouar mentions that, "in the vicinity of Itiyuru," people had spotted an Indian woman wearing one of the expedition's chronometers and an Indian man wearing Louis Billet's frock coat. Such information can throw suspicion on anyone: the Matacos of Itiyuru, the Chanés from the same place, or unidentified Indians who sold these objects—not to mention the accusations and contradictory information which circulated as fast as other objects on the Chaco frontier.

If, in July 1882, the Toba captains said that the Noctenes were in possession of the explorers' money, they also claimed that the Tobas from downriver were the killers and that the Güisnays of Piquirenda held the expedition's weapons. A month later, the same Tobas this time were accusing the Noctenes of the crime and maintaining that they had the weapons and the travelers' effects.

The great majority of amateur detectives at the time, and, consequently, the majority of written sources, do not for an instant doubt the Tobas' guilt in Crevaux's murder. Later information from Wagner, who purportedly encountered the murderer himself among the Tobas working on his property of Resistencia, in the Argentinian Chaco, and even the scam perpetrated later by Roger de Courteville, who accuses an old Toba sorcerer, point in the same direction.

A great many of the documents mention only anonymous, generic "Tobas," but others provide more details. According to Natalio Roldán, when the Tobas were discussing where to kill Crevaux and his men, "the headman, Oleoncito, or a similar name," was to blow his whistle as the signal. No one else mentions this odd name, and it may simply be a typographical error. On the other hand, the names of other Tobas are better known.

The first is a girl, almost a child: Yallá, accused immediately after the crime by the Gran Chaco subprefect. According to him, the murder was planned "as soon as the Toba girl taken from Tarija had been freed and told them everything they had taken with them and why they were

Figure 27. Toba Indians from Teyu (1903)
Photo by Jean-Baptiste Vaudry, in Combès and Salaun, *El Chaco de Jean-Baptiste Vaudry* (2018), p. 120.

traveling on the river."[1] But it was Yallá's duty as ambassadress to warn the Indians, and she cannot be reproached for fulfilling her mission. What the Tobas decided to do or not to do after having learned of the explorers' arrival is another story; nothing tells us if it was the girl who chose not to return, or if her parents forbade her. Neither Giannecchini nor Thouar, in his first account of 1884, accuses Yallá; they merely say that she did not return to the San Francisco mission. By contrast, in 1889 and again in 1891, imagining the dialogue between Yallá and the Pilcomayo Tobas, Thouar makes her indisputably guilty.

From the outset, the most frequently mentioned killer was Cuserai. The letter written June 8, 1882, by a Franciscan, claims that Crevaux met "Caserai" at Teyu; shortly afterward, the correspondent of the newspaper *El Trabajo* says the same thing, and Bernard Trigo, too, later writes that, when the expedition arrived in Teyu, "Cuzaray, captain of the Tobas and Noctenes," presented himself. We already know the disastrous background of this figure, who managed to unite Franciscan missionaries and Criollos, who for once found themselves sharing the same hatred. Whether or not he was guilty of killing Crevaux, Cuserai could not help being accused: he was the ideal culprit.

He appears several times flanked by other captains such as Peloco, who went with him to meet the Campos expedition at Santa Bárbara de Teyu in 1883, or Cutaicoliqui, who was with him the day he died at the Crevaux Settlement. Several of these Toba leaders presented themselves at the San Francisco mission in July and again in August 1882: first Iñiri, Cutaicoliqui, and Caligagae, accompanied a month later by Pelocoliqui-guazu.

Marcelleti, Giannecchini, and the Gran Chaco subprefect, Eudogio Raña, beseeched them to return the prisoners and the belongings stolen from the explorers: an indication that they were considered guilty beyond the shadow of a doubt. But these were leaders, and leaders who could have ordered the murder without actually doing it themselves. Whatever the case, it was Caligagae and Peloco who freed Francisco Zeballos, and it seems clear that they were more or less involved in the killing. According to the later testimony of José Correa, questioned in May 1886 by Thouar, Crevaux and his companions were killed "by old Peloko's Tobas." In 1906, Thouar repeats this claim and states that "Poloko's" men took an active part in the killing.

Caligagae is the father of the girl, Yallá. We also know that he is the son of a certain Icuru, who distinguished himself earlier, in the 1870s, as the leader of several attacks and thefts perpetrated at the San Francisco and San Antonio missions: Icuru was thus a comrade in arms of Cuserai, who had organized the Tobas' flight from the San Francisco mission in 1870. But Caligagae himself was already a captain at that time. He appears in a list drawn up by Fr. Marcelleti in 1877, which enumerates the Toba headmen present at the mission: Cuserai, head of fourteen families and fourteen soldiers; Iñiri, with fourteen families as well and sixteen soldiers; Calicagai, head of ten families and twelve soldiers; Guagua, twelve families and thirteen soldiers; and Chacari, six families and seven soldiers.[2]

Iñiri figures on this list, but the rest of the information I was able to gather on this captain is fairly sparse. He is probably the same Iñiri, or Niri, encountered by José Gianelli on his expedition in 1863, and who accompanied him to the San Francisco mission. Therefore, in 1882, he was elderly.

Under the names of Peloco, Pelocoliqui, Pelocoliqui-guaso, and other variants, the documents are probably talking about two people, perhaps a father and son, such as they appear in the novel by Théophile Novis. Indeed in 1883 the members of the Campos expedition describe Peloco as "a severe old man of 80 or 90, highly respected by his people," "almost

Figure 28. "Kali-gagae. Toba Captain, Father of the Indian Girl Yallá or Petrona"
Drawing by Théophile Novis (Archives Nationales, F/17/3009B, dossier Thouar).

blind, at least 95 years old," or disabled, blind, and over 80.[3] His camp stood downriver from Cabayurepoti. From what we know of his somewhat hectic life, Peloco seems to have adopted an ambiguous, unstable stance in his dealings with the *karai*. He shows up in the peace treaty of 1859 (under the name of "Pezocorique"), but in 1863, "Pelocolic" is described as a rebel, and flees the San Francisco mission; nevertheless, the same year, he is on good terms with the members of the Rivas/Gianelli expedition and even accompanies several sick Criollos as far as Itiyuru. However in 1876, we find a Peloco in Teyu and once again an enemy. In 1883, his attitude has once more changed, and he offers the Campos expedition peace as well as his own sons as guides.

Given the age of this figure, it is unlikely that the Pelocoliqui-guasu who presented himself at the San Francisco mission in 1882 is the same blind old man that the Campos expedition encountered a year later. This "big" (*guasu*) Peloco may be the son of the first, and it is probably he who appears again in 1887 at the end of the lamentable Thouar expedition. On this occasion, "Pelocolique-guasu" is identified as the captain of the Tobas from Taringuiti, across from Bella Esperanza. After Thouar had abandoned his men, the latter engaged Pelocoliqui-guasu to go in

Figure 29. "Pelloko-lik, Toba Captain"
Drawing by Théophile Novis (Archives Nationales, F/17/3009B, dossier Thouar).

search of him in exchange for an attractive reward: a cow, a horse, three machetes, two ponchos, an axe, three *arrobes* of maize flour, three of salt, and six packets of tobacco. Nevertheless, a few days later the Toba captain returned empty-handed, and his attitude toward the members of the expedition was no longer as cordial.[4]

As for Cutaicoliqui, if he appeared at this time as one leader among others, in the years that followed, he became the principal Indian opponent of colonization. Indeed, although the documents from the 1880s generally call him *Cu*taicoliqui or *Co*taicoliqui, two of them call him Taicolique or Taicorique. This is the case of Eudogio Raña when listing the Toba leaders who arrived at the San Francisco mission in August 1882 and of Giannecchini in his account of Cuserai's death. The other letters or reports recounting the same events speak of "Cutaicoliqui"; there is therefore no doubt that it is the same man. Probably younger than the other Toba leaders named in 1882 (he is not on Marcelleti's 1877 list), at the beginning of the twentieth century, Taicoliqui is the biggest Toba war chief in all Bolivia. Nordenskiöld observes that "the Toba leader Taycolique has no equal when it comes to supplying his people with guns."[5] Meanwhile Leocadio Trigo describes him as a man who is "astute and wise," and admits to Nordenskiöld that he is the only true leader, the only *big man* he has met on the Pilcomayo.[6] His exceptional role seems to have begun after the killing of Cuserai in 1883 and with (Cu)taicoliqui's revenge when he captured Cecilia Oviedo the following year. The Toba captain was not present at the signing of the peace treaty a few months later. He died in 1916 as he had lived, at Campo Durán in northwestern Argentina, killed by a Criollo.[7]

Taicoliqui does not exhaust the list of Toba suspects. Indeed Yallá was said to have denounced other guilty parties to Thouar (him again) in 1887. Their names are the following, with slight variation between Thouar's first account in 1889, his 1891 book, and his report dated 1899:

- Cuserai
- Cototo
- Suguai (Sugai in 1891)
- Cutiguasu
- Peloko
- Tasikii (Tasihii in 1891)

We are already familiar with the names of Cuserai and Peloco, as well as Cototo: like Cuserai, Cototo and his brother, Socó, had always caused trouble for the missionaries, and he, too, was an ideal culprit. Unlike Socó and Cuserai, however, killed by the *karai* in September 1882 and November 1883 respectively, Cototo came out better. In 1895 he was living in the Toba camp of Tayasuñanca.[8]

Alternatively, information on the other Tobas denounced by Yallá is scarce. Captain Suguai lived in Teyu in 1895 and was hostile to the missionaries.[9] Cutiguasu ("Big Cuti") was probably the Cutií whom the Gianelli expedition encountered in Teyu in 1863: in this case, he was a headman of "the greatest interest," who had fled from the San Francisco mission with Peloco only later to repent.[10] If this is indeed the same man, he was already of a certain age in 1882, like Peloco or Iñiri. The same can be said of Tasihii, who already appeared in 1859 among the signatories to the peace treaty with the whites. He reappears in 1863, along with Peloco and Cutiguasu, among the fugitives from the mission, and is also described as someone "of the greatest interest." In 1887 he was still alive, in the Yuarenda camp, between Teyu and Cabayurepoti.[11]

All of the Tobas mentioned lived on the Pilcomayo along the stretch between San Francisco upstream and Cabayurepoti downstream; as we have seen, several of them were already elderly in 1882. Although Thouar asserts that, at the Crevaux Settlement, other Tobas confirmed that the names given by Yallá were those of the killers, we have above all a list of captains and headmen. More than the names of the killers themselves, Yallá seems to have designated different Toba bands by their leader's name, just as José Correa spoke of "Old Peloco's Tobas."

Furthermore Thouar's testimony, arranged or invented, remains shaky and cannot be blindly accepted. Only Peloco and Cuserai (and Yallá herself) meet with a certain unanimity when it comes to accusations. However, Peloco and Caligagae organized Francisco Zeballos's liberation, and Yallá is said to have saved Haurat and Blanco from death on the spot. These ambiguities prevent us from accusing them of the killings without looking elsewhere. In all events, it seems clear that we cannot charge "the Tobas" with the crime: the "palaver" mentioned in the letter of June 8, 1882, also shows that the various Toba camps and bands were not necessarily working together and could not have come to a unanimously agreed plan for the murder or have decided the captives' fates.

In fact, the upstream Tobas, represented by Iñiri, Caligagae, and Cutaicoliqui in July 1882, denounced those downstream, and this accusation was not new: in 1859 already, suspected of having stolen some cattle, the Tobas in the vicinity of Teyu accused their "downstream kin" of the theft.[12] Clearly the killing of Crevaux was the occasion many seized upon to denounce their longtime enemies, and, coming precisely from leaders suspected of the crime, the accusation seems to lack some credibility. Nevertheless a few elements could partially confirm this. When Francisco Zeballos spoke to Fr. Marcelleti about the possibility of revenge on the part of the Güisnays—Sirome, for the murder of his father by a Criollo—he added other details: he asserted that the Tobas of Teyu and those of Cabayurepoti, downstream, were not in agreement about killing Crevaux—which would seem to confirm the truth of their having held a "palaver." Those from Cabayurepoti, Zeballos claimed, wanted to launch an all-out war on the missions and the haciendas, but they were purportedly stopped by those from Teyu. On the other hand, "all agreed on killing Martín Barroso." And as we saw, in 1881 this Criollo settler had come to an agreement with Sirome to establish a settlement at Piquirenda. This new foundation would have ultimately encircled the

Tobas and the Noctenes, catching them in a pincer movement between the settlement and the upstream missions. We can add that it was also Barroso who had captured Yallá, and therefore was not likely to have enjoyed much sympathy from her kin. According to Zeballos, in 1882 several Tobas, led by Peloco, went "to Itiyuru pretending to be friends with Martín in order to take him to Cabayurepoti and kill him because they did not want Christians setting foot on their lands."[13] If this was the case, José Correa's statement accusing "old Peloko's Tobas of having recently arrived from a trip to Itiyuru" would make perfect sense. It could thus be thought that the Tobas from Cabayurepoti had decided to kill Crevaux to slow Barroso's planned advance, whereas those from Teyu would have preferred to await another opportunity, perhaps for fear of the outcry it would provoke. In this event, the guilty parties would effectively be the Tobas "from downstream," but not too far downstream: simply from around Cabayurepoti, downstream from Teyu.

Although the list of Toba suspects (from upstream or downstream) is already long, they are not—far from it—the only Indians accused of massacring the Crevaux expedition. At one time or another, all of the groups on the Pilcomayo were accused of having taken part in the murder.

Thus the list of suspects goes on, with the Chiriguanos, and more specifically the "defectors" or the mestizos, like Cototo, who lived outside the missions. According to the letter of June 8, Crevaux met Cuserai in Teyu, where he was accompanied by "a large number of Tobas and Chiriguanos." And Eudogio Raño, too, accuses the Chiriguanos together with the Tobas. Nor are the Chiriguano neophytes or the peons working on the Criollo haciendas exempt from all suspicion: as we know, Iramaye, from the Tigüipa mission, and Yahuanahua, sent from Caiza, were also accused of complicity.

In addition to the Chiriguanos, the "Tapietes," too, are possible killers—here we do not know if the documents are referring to the Nivaclés from downstream or the Guarani-speaking Tapietes. Whatever the case, in 1882 Raña puts them in the same sack as the Tobas and the Chiriguanos, and accuses them of the crime. Likewise, one Tarija newspaper wrote that, in May 1882, "persons arriving from the Gran Chaco" reported Crevaux distributing gifts to the "Tapietes."[14]

To the Tapietes, we must add the Güisnays, who, by killing Crevaux, could have been avenging the death of Sirome's father, and the Noctenes, since we have seen that Bernardo Trigo makes Cuserai a "captain of Tobas and Noctenes." We can assume that the "Indian scum" composed of Tobas and "part of the Neptons [sic]," who, according to Roldán, attacked Crevaux, refers to the Noctenes. The reference to Toba leaders gathered at the San Francisco mission in August 1882 is more explicit. The very persons who, a month earlier, had accused the downstream Tobas, now change culprits and instead indict a few more groups: "They replied that they had come to make peace, that those who had killed Crevaux were the Noctenes led by Tatuyuruy Blanco, who were presently in Itiyuru; that they had killed them a short distance upstream from Piquirenda, because the Tapietes and the Noctenes did not want Christians reaching the Paraguay."[15] In a letter writted by Raña and published in the newspapers, the names vary slightly; in this case, the guilty parties are "the Noctenes led by Tatoyuro and Blanco, who are now in Itiyuru." According to the subprefect, the Tobas also claimed (as proof of their innocence) to have saved Francisco Zeballos from these Noctenes and conducted him to the San Francisco mission.[16]

The motley list of presumed culprits is topped off by the Mataguayos from the right bank of the Pilcomayo, accused in 1906 by Thouar of having captured Haurat and having killed him on orders from the Tobas and the Chorotes, until now among the innocent; but an ill-informed article accuses them of having taken the survivors of the massacre prisoner.[17]

The finishing touch to the list of killers is the mysterious and nonexistent "Tape Chico" tribe. In effect, the telegram sent to the Argentinian newspaper, *La Nación*, by Francisco Arraya on May 28, 1882, reports: "The Tape Chico tribe welcomed the explorers with enthusiastic demonstrations of friendship only to go on to kill them."[18]

In addition to designating culprits whose names do not exist, this telegram was repeated with errors by several authors who did little to clarify the situation. Cutolo transforms these killers into "Tobas or Guaycurús from the Tape Chico tribe" (which could designate either a place or a leader), while Barnadas speaks of Tobas (but not Guaycurús) *from the* Tape Chico—even though the telegram does not mention Tobas.

Tape Chico can be excluded as a toponym because Arraya's telegram clearly states that the crime was committed at "Tello," that is Teyu. There is a slight possibility that Arraya was alluding to Cuserai himself: indeed as we have seen, this Toba's name is probably formed with the Guarani adjective *-rai*, which means "little" (*chico* in Spanish). Arraya may have been familiar with the idiomatic "*tape*," frequently used in the region of Corrientes and the Argentinian northwest; there, "*Tape*" (from the name given during colonial times to the Indian groups in the region) means "Indian," "someone who looks like an Indian." Should this be the case, Tape Chico would be the little (*chico* or *-rai*) Indian. But this interpretation is merely a possibility and another reading is more plausible, I would even say probable: the "Tape Chico" could be the "Tapietes." This is in all events what is suggested by the affirmation of Dr. Zeballos, of the Argentinian Geographic Institute; in July 1882 he writes that, *according to a telegram from Bolivia*, the explorers arrived in the territory of the "Tapeti [*sic*] Indians" and that it is they who were the killers.[19] If, as everything suggests, the telegram in question is that sent by Arraya, one might perhaps imagine a printing error on the part of *La Nación*.

Whatever the case, the specter of possible, probable, or potential Indian killers of Crevaux looms large, and covers all of the ethnic groups in the region. Because the Indians lied and accused their longtime enemies; because, for foreigners, an Indian was an Indian, whether he was a Toba on one page and a Noctene on the next; because, for the Criollos, the fierce Tobas were necessarily guilty of every evil. But also because Crevaux, the great Crevaux, could have died only if he were vastly outnumbered, and because it was impossible to believe that the hero could have been killed by a mere handful of savages. Which also explains the assertions of several early authors: at Cabayurepoti, the explorers found a large number of Indians from different ethnic groups, and "all of the tribes came to an agreement together to sacrifice Doctor Crevaux and his crew."[20] It is true that the ethnic kaleidoscope in the region and the fact that Cabayurepoti was a "general headquarters" or a "meeting point" for the groups in the Pilcomayo can point in this direction. Nevertheless this does not enable us to identify any more accurately those guilty of the crime, nor does it allow us to accuse "the Tobas" or rather "*all* of the Tobas." Their dispute with those of Teyu and their plans to kill Martín Barroso to slow colonization make those of Peloco the more likely suspects, but here, too, there is no truly incontrovertible proof.

With or without the complicity of Yallá, Iramaye, or Yahuanahua, the Tobas, the Noctenes, or other "Tape Chico" are in all events the material authors of the crime. For several chroniclers, they are also the sole intellectual authors of the killings: this is the case of those who speak of the "palaver" between Tobas that decided the explorers' fate. It is true of Raña, too, who maintains in his report of May 6 that the Indians planned everything in advance. It is also the case of someone like the Frenchman, Gustave Marguin, member of the August 1882 Fontana expedition, who thought that the Indians took fright when they saw the Bolivian and Argentinian military uniforms of Crevaux's companions, and that was the reason they attacked.[21]

But other authors do not share this point of view, and maintain that the Indians were driven to the murder by unidentified, shadowy figures who would thus be the real instigators of the crime, its intellectual authors, or its immediate causes: "doubt, horrible doubt remains as to the causes of this disaster; rumors, at first muffled, then more consistent, were proffered daily: the word 'murder' was pronounced; calls went out to discover the authors, to punish them."[22]

"When news of the massacre first broke, there was only one voice on the Bolivian border that accused the mission fathers of having prepared this horrible murder."[23] As we have seen on several occasions, the frontier settlers were not slow to denounce the missionaries as the intellectual authors of the massacre. Among all of the Franciscans on the frontier, the main person accused was, naturally, their leader, Doroteo Giannecchini. In his report written in 1899, in which he reiterates his accusations against the Franciscan, Thouar cites as proof letters written by frontier Criollos. One of these denounces the missionaries for having always been hostile to settlers and even claims they encouraged the Indians to rob and attack them:

This outcry, which has been growing for four years, is on the lips of all those skilled in remaining silent, and those who think have always judged that the missionaries were the authors of the massacre of Crevaux, of Colonel Rivas's forces, of the theft of his 250 horses ... The missionaries' ambition, in their will to dominate the Chaco by means of their machinations exercised on the Tobas against all attempts at progress, settlement, exploration, etc., etc., is known by all ... The Chaco would prosper if it had a township alongside each mission, set up openly and provided with magistrates and schoolmasters.[24]

Another missive comes from a Frenchman established on the Parapeti River north of the Pilcomayo, Alexandre Lelarge, who warns Thouar to be wary of the Franciscans. In his 1889 and 1890 publications, Thouar had mentioned this letter without transcribing it:

Beware of tricks and hypocrisy. I said the same thing to Mr. Crevaux in Tarairi, as well as to Mr. Billet in Caiza; my advice was not heeded; it is true that trust is a characteristic trait of the French, and Mr. Crevaux, brimming with boldness and full of trust in the missionaries, did not take the precautions he should have, even though he had been warned ... But what is one to do? He paid dearly for this trust, and his death will always be a mystery.[25]

In the same report, Thouar claims that Crevaux and his men were perfectly armed and could have held out against the Indians, but that perfidious advice from Giannecchini persuaded them to leave their weapons packed in the bottom of the boats. Yallá would have known about this, according to Thouar, and warned the Tobas that "the Gringos" were not going to open fire; but that, too, does not jibe with Francisco Zeballos's testimony, according to which it was Crevaux himself who had the weapons stowed away so as not to frighten the Indians. Whatever the case, Théophile Novis, Thouar's companion and later brother-in-law, tells the same story: "It can seem surprising that these men did not defend themselves. Here is the reason: Father Doroteo had recommended they proceed with caution and avoid using guns. In order to avoid an incident, Crevaux had them kept locked away in a box made for this purpose."[26]

Other, later authors repeated the same accusation, probably because they had read Thouar's texts. For instance, according to L.-D. Wagner, "the Tobas were excited and urged to kill" by other persons, and the killer himself is reported to have told him that "he was driven to act in this way by the Bolivian missionaries," who, he says, "told him: 'A White man will soon come to cast a spell on you, he will not be armed, but he and his troop will wave green branches to incite the Evil Spirits to attack you.'"[27] And in 1936, once again, a German, Helmuth Kanter, maintained that the explorers were killed on orders from Doroteo Giannecchini.[28]

But the reality is that the accusation is not supported by proof, and it does not lead to any legal action against the Franciscans. Nor do the fiercest liberals of the time, like Daniel Campos, who devoted long pages of his book to harsh criticism of the missions, allude to the friars' supposed guilt. This accusation is therefore not very convincing either. Just as the Tobas upstream denounce those living downstream, or the Noctenes, the Criollos use the Crevaux case to suit their own purposes and make up accusations to fit. Thouar, too, has his own—very different—interests, and takes advantage of the accusation against the Franciscans to excuse his own failure.

As additional "evidence," Thouar includes in his report two letters written by Giannecchini to his brothers in religion at the time of the 1887 expedition. In one of these, the Franciscan shows little enthusiasm for the exploration in which he is participating:

This exploration is the final sentence for the Tobas and other Indians, as well as for the missions: for, if the Indians help us to get through and do not fight us, they will be recommended to the Government for the establishment of a mission or, better, they will be grouped together to work for entrepreneurs: otherwise they will be condemned to extermination, and local or foreign immigration will replace them. So, what about our missions? ... We will soon find out! Thouar himself said it: this expedition will resolve the Toba-Pilcomayo-Chaco problem. The temptation almost, almost comes to me, as I arrive in Buenos Aires, to retire, despite my great age, to Tuscany, for I could not suffer seeing the missions die or these places awash in blood and filled with atheists or infidels worse than the Tobas.[29]

If this declaration "proves" something, it is in all events not Giannecchini's hand in the murder of Crevaux. Alternatively, it can show the discouragement prompted by the disastrous expedition of 1887, or the missionaries' disillusionment. In 1887 as well as in 1882, it is probable that the friars did not favor an expedition that would necessarily facilitate the arrival of greater numbers of new settlers; it is possible that they sought to protect their influence along the downstream stretch of the Pilcomayo; it is also possible that they were unwilling to obey the regulations obliging them to cooperate with attempts at exploring the Pilcomayo. But the disagreement ultimately bears more on the methods used than on the legitimacy of the *karai* penetration of the Chaco. Settlers, authorities, and Franciscans alike assumed the existence of an "Indian problem," and all believed themselves capable of turning the natives into a source of cheap labor, at last "integrated" and of use to the nation. There were disagreements first of all over competition for access to manual labor between missions and haciendas, and then concerning the other suggestions for solving the "Indian problem." To the settlers' proposal to purely and simply exterminate unsubjugated Indians, the Franciscans responded with the watchwords "civilization" and "Christianization," which in the event are synonymous—and it is no accident if the "Whites" and the settlers are the "Christians" in the documents of the time. But even though they set themselves up as the natives' defenders and protectors, the missionaries needed the settlement movement, the expeditions that went with it, and the military forts that favored its expansion. They were quick to collaborate in this type of enterprise, as shown by Gianelli in 1863. In the end, the best "proof" of Giannecchini's innocence in the Crevaux affair is his second letter, intercepted by his fiercest detractor. Observing the agitation of the Pilcomayo Indians as the expedition passed, the Franciscan wrote: "God willing that it does not go with us as with Crevaux in the wake of the Caiza people's expedition."[30] Admittedly this is not the type of reflection one might expect of someone suspected of being the intellectual author of the murder.

We must remember, too, that, unlike the Tobas (and certainly the majority of the Criollos), the Italian friars knew perfectly well who Jules Crevaux was, and that he had been recommended by the French, Argentinian, and Bolivian governments. In other words, they knew that his disappearance would not go unremarked and would have serious consequences. Furthermore, and even if the missionaries enjoyed a certain prestige among the unsubjugated Indians, it is highly unlikely that this influence was great enough to convince the indomitable Tobas to expose themselves, as they had done, to the Criollos' revenge.

In their own defense, the Franciscans also accused the Caiza people's expedition against the Indians shortly before Crevaux's departure for points downstream. Those who accuse him, Giannecchini says, are actually the guilty parties or, at least, those who incited the Indians to massacre.

Contrary to the missionaries' denunciations, which were aimed directly at Giannecchini, the accusations bearing on the Franciscans spoke only of generic Criollos, without naming names. But it must be acknowledged, too, that there exists no tangible proof against them. Thouar, who in 1884 accuses them of espousing the Franciscans' viewpoint, later changes his mind and declares them innocent: indeed, the Indians they killed or captured in March 1882 were Noctenes, and "the Toba Indians ... not having had to suffer from the people of Caiza, had therefore no reason to exact revenge" (Thouar takes this opportunity to assert that, therefore, the Tobas were incited to kill by a Franciscan hand).[31] But this is not a real argument either. Even if the captives were Noctenes, we do not know if any Tobas numbered among the dead, and what we do know of the inextricable ethnic patchwork on the Pilcomayo does not allow us to reach a conclusion. Nor was the March 1882 expedition the only one undertaken by the people of Caiza, and the Tobas could just as well have wanted to avenge earlier deaths.

But the Franciscans were not the only ones to suggest that the frontier Criollos were guilty or complicit. There where Giannecchini designates them as "immediate causes" of Crevaux's death, others see them as the instigators of the crime. Some hint at a possible direct link between the killings and the incident at Tumbaya in January 1882. Such is the insinuation of the French newspaper, *La Revue alsacienne*, in 1882, and a year later Thouar also recommends "keeping in mind the incident that happened on the Argentinian-Bolivian border, where, when an Argentinian sailor fired his revolver, the explorers were attacked by twelve individuals."[32] Yet unless, as the French papers suggested, the motive of the crime was the money unwisely shown by Crevaux on this occasion, the connection with the expedition's massacre is not really clear. In the end, even if the incident may have exacerbated sensitivities, it was Crevaux himself who incurred the most problems at Tumbaya, and not the local population.

Later, in 1910, the same Wagner who had cited a Toba headman as accusing the Franciscans also expresses his doubts. For him, if the Tobas were incited to kill by a third party, this could well have been the local authorities (settlers, in other words), who feared that Crevaux's trip might reveal contraband activity. In this case, Yahuanahua would have been sent by the Criollos to verify that the killing had indeed taken place and not to gather information on the explorers. But once again, we have no proof.

There is not much danger of error if we suppose that the explorations and expeditions, like that of Crevaux, encouraged by the government, were not to the taste of the frontier settlers, far from major centers and generally living by their own laws. The Criollos often refused to sign up for the expeditions and, even if Thouar exaggerates in his denunciations, those living in the Isoso did not do much to help. But from there to planning and carrying out (or having the Indians carry out) the murder of some twenty people, the means seem disproportionate and, in the end, futile. The Bolivian government considered sending expeditions to the Chaco before Crevaux arrived, and would have done so anyway. But more convincing than any argument is the fact that several members of the massacred crew were their friends, their neighbors, or their kin, which speaks in favor of the Criollos' innocence.

The mutual accusations flung between settlers and Franciscans led to nothing. They were as much accusations as means of defense, and, in the latter case, Crevaux's death seems to have served above all as a pretext to rekindle old grudges and rivalries. The best way to find the guilty parties is still to ask who benefited from the crime.

In the end, it matters little whether the killers were savage Indians, sinister Italian Franciscans, or cruel Bolivian settlers; Crevaux did not die for what he was, but for what he represented. Whether the expedition members were killed in revenge for the Caiza expedition, to avenge the death of the father of the headman, Sirome, or to slow the foundation of the new settlement at Piquirenda planned by Martín Barroso, in all cases, the explorers died as innocent victims of a vendetta with which they had nothing to do. But vengeance is not always wreaked on those directly responsible for a death or a killing; it can also fall on their relatives, their band, their allies. Crevaux and his companions were white men, they represented the Criollos, they were suitable targets for revenge.

If there was someone who did not benefit from the crime, it was the Indians on the Pilcomayo. The Tobas' already well-established reputation for fierceness could only grow with the news of the killings. The chapter Baldrich devotes in 1890 to the Pilcomayo Indians begins with these lines:

> Here we have finally come to the last stage of our work and we are now facing the Toba Indians, Crevaux's killers, the scourge of the Bolivian villages in the Central and Northern Chaco, plundered and attacked by them from time immemorial, and bulwark against which the military operations of this republic, like that of Rivas, have collided.[33]

Eudogio Raña had already laid out the program for years to come in his first report on the killings:

> These savages will never abandon their natural habit and the profession that has been theirs ever since the inhabitants of the Argentinian Chaco and this whole province have known them; their habit and their profession are idleness, wandering, theft, treachery, and murder ... it has been impossible to subdue them by gentle methods, and these savages will always be the eternal enemies of Christians, progress, and civilization, and consequently responsible for the underdevelopment and the ruin of these emerging villages. These savage men cannot be considered as human beings, but as tigers and panthers, and as such they must be hunted down, because they are of use only to themselves, not to humanity, or society, or the state. For this reason, the government, so as to protect the security of the property and the life of these inhabitants, is obliged to order the four provinces of Azero, Cordillera, Salinas, and Gran Chaco to organize an expedition every four months until these savage nations have been wiped out.[34]

And it is a fact that the expeditions increased over the months and years following the massacre. In July 1882 Fontana set out from Argentina;

Rivas did likewise from Bolivia in October of the same year; and Ibaceta and Compos left in 1883, representing their respective governments. True they explored, but they were also responding to a cry for vengeance echoed thousands of times in the newspapers of the time: "Barbarity has killed civilization; ignorance has extinguished light … Revenge!, cries science, civilization, and progress; Revenge! Industry and trade repeat with them"; "Humanity itself clamors for the extinction of these accursed savages who hold back civilization's triumphant chariot," and so on.[35] Military settlements and manhunts were the fruit of the Tobas' acts, or more generally of those of all of the Chaco Indians. In the decades that followed, the Tobas would gradually be driven from Bolivian territory, and would leave for good shortly before the Chaco War.

More than any specific settlers or missionaries, Crevaux's death benefited the settlement movement itself. It became yet another pretext to justify, to legitimize, the march forward. Contemporaries formulated this profession of faith in myriad ways: "This sacrifice should henceforth become a program: the extinguishing of barbarity at the heart of America"; "The sacrifice and murder of the heroic explorers, Creveaux [*sic*] and Ibarreta … showed the way for civilizing action."[36]

Once again the figures of Crevaux and Ibarreta merge, and their deaths encourage the conquest and the definitive colonization of the Chaco: "the interest Enrique de Ibarreta's exploration aroused among the authorities and in public opinion sowed the idea in army headquarters of the definitive conquest of the Chaco."[37] Government-financed exploratory expeditions like that of Crevaux are the means of, or the obligatory preludes to, colonization. As one Alsatian magazine said: they are called to render service to the whole world, for such "travelers are the quartermasters of the human race; they open the way and mark every stage."[38] But the Tobas and other Indians are excluded from "the whole world" and the "human race," and they know it. Opening a path of communication between Bolivia and Paraguay via the Pilcomayo "is something they detest wholeheartedly, because they know full well that they will be forced to forsake their lands, their savage freedom, and their trade as thieves."[39]

Jules Crevaux, the mythical "barefoot explorer," was perfectly aware of his role as vanguard of "civilization." On the subject of his earlier travels in Amazonia and Guyana, Francis Grandhomme observes:

When he evokes the natural resources and the agricultural production of the regions visited, Crevaux systematically retains things that may be of some interest ... Indeed Crevaux is animated as much by the search for riverheads as the navigability of rivers and tributaries, and reminds his successors to take into consideration the weather conditions, the practicability of rivers during the dry season, or suggests a method of approaching and bypassing falls ... Yet this advice is not meant for explorers in the immediate future but rather for future landowners and merchants. In the Guianas, already in navigating up the Maroni or the Oyapock Rivers, Crevaux sought to establish or to facilitate the exploitation of both forests and gold-bearing zones. More generally, he described commercial access and outlets.[40]

The explorer probably had economic interests in Guyana, perhaps in a mining company. In any event, his contemporaries regarded him as an agent of civilization and an asset for the newly discovered territories. Let us not forget that, before leaving for the Pilcomayo, Crevaux had also proposed another project to the Bolivian government, one for exploring the upper Purus, on the northwest border of the country; this territory, too, was the object of international dispute and would ultimately pass under Peruvian control in 1909.[41]

Crevaux was a man of his time and a firm believer in the necessary and beneficial march of progress and colonization. He criticized the "collateral" effects of colonization such as corruption, acculturation, deforestation, or the epidemics which decimated the Indians, but he did not question its necessity. From this standpoint, he is much closer to a Giannecchini than to a Raña and, in fact, a month before his death, he wrote to the Tarija prefect: "My thanks to the Reverend Franciscan Fathers who contributed so effectively to the cause of the civilization of Bolivia."[42] Likewise we read in his last letter to the Bolivian Minister of Finances and Industry: "The role of these modest fathers is much more important than is generally thought. Have they not rendered a great service to Bolivia by winning 10,000 barbarians to civilization?"[43] The methods and the means can be questioned and fiercely criticized; the "cause of civilization," never.

Upon learning of the death of Crevaux and his companions, the inhabitants of Tarija exclaimed: "They died for the sake of Science, Bolivia, and humanity";[44] his friend, the explorer Francisco Moreno, saw the victims as "martyrs of civilization and victims of barbarity."[45] Like Ibarreta, Crevaux "died a valiant champion of progress."[46] On April 27, 1899, exactly seventeen years after Crevaux's death, Miguel Ortiz, a companion of Ibarreta's, wrote a posthumous letter to his friend: "You died at the hands of those to whom you were trying to impart a glimmer of civilization, bringing as much glory to your name as a vast field to be conquered, thanks to your knowledge."[47]

Martyrs to science, Crevaux and Ibarreta were also martyrs to civilization, which in this case and at the time were the same thing. Science and knowledge were at the service of colonization or, in a more humanistic version, of "civilization." A perhaps recalcitrant champion of the former, Crevaux was a staunch defender of the latter. If his name remains immortalized on the banks of the Pilcomayo, it is in the form of a military settlement, "a new population center there where the savage element once reigned."[48]

In all likelihood, the immediate reason the explorers were murdered was the expedition organized by the people of Caiza in March 1882, or the death of Sirome's father, or Martín Barroso's intention to found a settlement at Piquirenda. But we cannot affirm that, in the absence of these concrete motives, nothing would have happened. Perhaps not in that specific place nor on that date, and perhaps with other Indians from downriver, like the "Tapietes" who had gallantly fought against Campos in 1883. In all events, the Tobas, or the Indians in general, were not mistaken about their victim. Crevaux died for the sake of the colonization he personified, just as Cuserai was accused for the desperate resistance he embodied.

Epilogue

Sometimes one feels a need to get to the bottom of things…
Unanswered questions can hang on and on.
Henning Mankell, *Firewall*

The massacre of the Crevaux mission is a fact, but it ultimately became a myth—the Crevaux myth—or, who knows, a tragicomedy. It is the story of survivors who died and of dead men who survived; of two skulls for a single victim; of three crime scenes for a single crime. It is a novel featuring the appearance of one (or two) perfidious interpreters, an anonymous cook, suspicious friars, and fake detectives, a recalcitrant Toba who could only have been guilty, accused innocents, and insane witnesses, suspects guilty of stammering or of murder. It is the story of a massacre somewhere on the hazy border marked by a river disputed by three countries and belonging to none. It is also the story of a never-ending cycle of vengeance: one Crevaux for the Noctenes killed by the Caiza settlers, or for the father of Sirome; a Cuserai for a Crevaux; a Cecilia Oviedo for a Cuserai. Even if, from this standpoint, the settlers might appear to be just one more combatant in the Pilcomayo wars, the difference is huge compared with conflicts between Indians proper: this time the very survival of the Indigenous groups is at stake, their freedom, and their territory.

The motive for the crime is no doubt the easiest to understand, and the most understandable. Jules Crevaux set out in the service of three countries and of "civilization." He died because none of these countries had achieved control of the Indigenous Chaco. Even if this was not the only cause, Crevaux's death was a trigger or a pretext for the advance of the colonization and conquest of this region. Instead of the twelve-meter-high column that the colony's founders had planned as a tribute to the French explorer, the French embassy in Bolivia has recently erect-ed a bust of Crevaux on the square of the ex-military settlement, today a Weenhayek (formerly Noctene) village. One of the residents pointed it out to me, explaining that it was "a monument to those who had died in the [Chaco] War," and he was not all that wrong. Crevaux's exploratory expeditions, his death, and the fallout are an element of the prelude to this deadly war which obliterated the ethnic landscape of the Pilcomayo and left the flags of Bolivia and Paraguay flying over a once all-Indian Chaco.

The names of the actual killers, the exact place of the crime, the cir-cumstances surrounding the killing are all lost in time, probably forever. So what precisely do we know? Very little. The date of the crime—April 27, 1882, is established— not the time, but we can do without this detail. The members of the mission numbered seventeen, providing we assume that Iramaye and Chiriqui are the same person. The killing was carried out in the vicinity of Cabayurepoti and not Teyu, and probably some-where downstream from Cabayurepoti. The travelers seem to have been clubbed to death, using traditional Toba weapons, as most of the docu-ments state. And the bodies were left lying on the bank, with no trace of cannibalism, without a funeral ceremony, no festive drinking from their skulls or their scalps.

The killers were Indians and very probably Tobas, but it is more com-plicated to give them a name and a face. Cuserai is too emblematic a figure for us to blindly accept the accusations against him. Peloco seems the most likely suspect, but others like Caligagae or Iñiri, who guided Francisco Zeballos to the San Francisco mission, are not free of suspi-cion. Likewise Yallá naturally warned her father and his fellow tribes-men of the explorers' arrival—that was her role—but no doubt not in the terms reported by Thouar. We are not certain whether the killing of April 1882 was the outcome of a plot conceived in advance (like the intention to kill Martín Barroso or that to avenge Sirome's father) or something that occurred without premeditation, for example when the distribution of gifts degenerated or, as the Indians told the missionary Grubb, because an expedition member provoked them. The participation of other Indians than the Tobas is still an unknown, but it is not unlikely: the Tobas' ties with the Chiriguanos or with mestizos like Cototo make their participation a likelihood, and the story of the Caiza settlers' expedition or the killing of Sirome's father allow us to envisage the presence of Noctenes or Güisnays as well.

On the other hand, there is no hard evidence that would implicate either the Franciscans or the Criollos of Caiza and Yacuiba. Even if the expedition organized in March by the latter incited the Indians to revenge, they cannot be accused of having planned a massacre in which several of their own fell. Finally and no doubt possibly, the settlers were also right in accusing Crevaux's lack of lucidity and the excessive trust he placed in the Indians and in his own capabilities as a negotiator.

That is all we have—and even this recapitulation is full of "maybe," "perhaps," and "probably." So these pages are, and must remain, incomplete. Their only merit is perhaps to have gathered all of the documents into a single volume. But the exercise was worthwhile. If I have managed to clarify something about the Crevaux affair, it is that nothing is clear; it is the fact that writing the story also means listening to stories. The mystery surrounding Crevaux's death and the myths that grew up around it make it a veritable textbook case.

Cui bono? Who benefits from the crime? The colonization of the Chaco? Yes, but also at the cost of manipulations and exaggerations. The settlers who thus justified hunting down "the tigers and the panthers" of the Pilcomayo? The Franciscans now able to criticize the settlers? It even benefited Arthur Thouar, who was not present but who clung to Crevaux's shadow in order to garner his own laurels or excuse his own pitiful failures. From the outset then, the testimonies of those closest to the affair—what historians call "primary sources"—all give rise to confusion, contradictions, exaggerations, lies, inventions, or manipulations. In every case, testimonies are altered and "facts" boil down to self-serving or unconscious lies: the Tobas are the killers simply because these can only be Tobas. Relying on such "firsthand" sources—or more generally on secondhand accounts—the subsequent literature only deepens the mystery and multiplies the contradictions, creating a snowball effect.

Nothing was lacking in Crevaux's death to place it more in the realm of fantasy than of history. The murder itself has been forgotten, and with it the flesh-and-blood victims. The aura surrounding Crevaux has overshadowed the figures of his fellow travelers and their deaths. There is no agreement as to their names or their number. In the engravings published of the massacre—for lack of photos— the explorer faces his savage killers alone or nearly alone. But in the long run, he, too, has disappeared behind his myth. In the end, no one has really taken an interest in what actually happened on that April 27, 1882. All that remains are the pretexts, the excuses, the justifications, the denunciations, and fertile ground for morbid imaginings and mediocre writing. All that remains is the mystery.

Selected Bibliography

Archives

ABNB   Archivo y Biblioteca Nacionales de Bolivia (Sucre)
- MG: Ministerio de la Guerra
- MH: Ministerio de Hacienda
- MI: Ministerio del Interior
- MSS: Manuscritos

AFT   Archivo Franciscano de Tarija
- Archivo Corvera
- Complemento del archivo Corvera

AHT   Archivo Histórico de Tarija
- PR: Prefectura de Tarija

AN   Archives Nationales de France (Paris)

AVL   Private archives of Virginio Lema Trigo (Tarija)

BNF   Bibliothèque Nationale de France (Paris)

CDL   Casa de la Libertad (Sucre)

Anon. 1884. "The Crevaux Expedition." *Science* 3 (60).

Asp, Otto. 1905. *Expedición al Pilcomayo. 27 de marzo–6 de octubre de 1903*. Buenos Aires: Publicaciones de la oficina meteorológica argentina, Anales del Ministerio de Agricultura, vol. 1, no. 1.

Aurois, Claude, and Alain Monnier, eds. 1998. *De Suiza a Sudamérica. Etnologías de Alfred Métraux*. Geneva: Museum of Ethnography.

Baldrich, Amadeo. 1890. *Las Comarcas vírgenes. El Chaco central norte*. Buenos Aires/La Plata: Jacobo Peuser.

Barbier, Joseph-Victor. 1899. "Préface." In *Trente mois au continent mystérieux*, by Jean-François Payeur-Didelot, v–xi. Paris/Nancy: Berger-Levrault.

Barnadas, Josep. 2002. "Crevaux, Jules." In *Diccionario histórico de Bolivia*, vol. 1, edited by Josep Barnadas, 631. Sucre: Grupo de Estudios Históricos.

Borges, Jorge Luis. 1996. "El Cuento policial." In *Obras completas*, vol. 4, 189–97. Barcelona: Emecé.

Bossert, Federico. 2012. "Notas sobre la jerarquía interétnica en los ingenios azucareros del noroeste argentino." In *Las Tierras bajas de Bolivia: Miradas históricas y antropológicas*, edited by Diego Villar and Isabelle Combès, 217–36. Santa Cruz: El País/Museo de Historia de la UAGRM.

Braunstein, José. 2006. "El signo del agua. Formas de clasificación étnica wichí." In *Definiciones étnicas, organización social y estrategias políticas en el Chaco y la Chiquitania*, edited by Isabelle Combès, 145–53. Lima: Institut Français d'Études Andines/Santa Cruz de la Sierra: El País–SNV Bolivia.

Bresson, André. 1886. *Bolivia. Sept années d'explorations, de voyages et de séjours dans l'Amérique australe*. Paris: Challamel.

Broc, Numa. 1982a. "Les Explorateurs français au XIXe siècle reconsidérés." *Revue française d'Histoire d'Outre-Mer* 69 (256): 237–73.

———. 1982b. "Les Explorateurs français au XIXe siècle reconsidérés (suite)." *Revue française d'Histoire d'Outre-Mer* 69 (257): 323–59.

———. 1999. *Dictionnaire illustré des explorateurs et grands voyageurs français du XIXe siècle*, vol. 3: *Amérique*. Paris: CTHS.

Calzavarini, Lorenzo, ed. 2006. *Presencia franciscana y formación intercultural en el sudeste de Bolivia según documentos del archivo franciscano de Tarija 1606–1936*. Tarija: Centro Eclesial de Documentación.

Campos, Daniel. 1888. *De Tarija a la Asunción. Expedición boliviana de 1883*. Buenos Aires: Jacobo Peuser.

Chaumeil, Jean-Pierre. 2009. "Primeros clichés. Las Tribulaciones del doctor Crevaux en la Amazonía." In *Entre textos e imágenes. Representaciones antropológicas de la América indígena*, edited by Fermín del Pino-Díaz, Pascal Riviale, and Juan J. R. Villarías-Robles, 213–25. Madrid: CSIC.

Coello de la Rosa, Alexandre, and Josep Lluís Mateo Dieste. 2020. *In Praise of Historical Anthropology: Perspectives, Methods and Applications to the Study of Power and Colonialism*. New York: Routledge.

146

Combès, Isabelle. 2005. *Etno-historias del Isoso. Chané y chiriguanos en el Chaco boliviano (siglos XVI–XX)*. La Paz: Institut Français d'Études Andines.

———, ed. 2006. *Definiciones étnicas, organización social y estrategias políticas en el Chaco y la Chiquitania*. Lima: Institut Français d'Études Andines/ Santa Cruz de la Sierra: El País–SNV Bolivia.

———. 2016. *Historia del pérfido Cuñamboy. La Cordillera chiriguana en los albores de la independencia de Bolivia*. Cochabamba: Itinerarios – ILAMIS, Scripta autochtona, 16.

———. 2019. *Hijos del Pilcomayo. Los últimos tobas de Bolivia*. Cochabamba: Itinerarios.

Combès, Isabelle, and Michèle Salaun, eds. 2018. *El Chaco de Jean-Baptiste Vaudry*. Sucre: ABNB.

Combès, Isabelle, Diego Villar, and Kathleen Lowrey. 2009. "Comparative Studies and the South American Gran Chaco." *Tipiti: Journal of the Society for the Anthropology of Lowland South America* 7 (1): 69–102.

Corrado, Alejandro. 1884. "Continuación de la historia del Colegio franciscano de Tarija." In *El Colegio franciscano de Tarija y sus misiones. Noticias históricas recogidas por dos misioneros del mismo Colegio*, 279–503, edited by Antonio Comajuncosa and Alejandro Corrado. Quaracchi: Colegio de San Buenaventura.

Crevaux, Jules. 1987. *Le Mendiant de l'Eldorado. De Cayenne aux Andes, 1876–1879*. Paris: Phébus. Reissue of *Voyages dans l'Amérique du Sud*. Paris: Hachette, 1883.

Cutolo, Osvaldo Vicente. 1969. "Crevaux, Julio." In *Nuevo diccionario biográfico argentino (1750–1930)*, vol. 2, 405–406. Buenos Aires: Elche.

Díez Arguedas, Julio. 1971. *Expedicionarios y exploradores del suelo boliviano*. La Paz: Camarlinghi.

Ducci, Zacarías. 1895. *Diario de la visita a todas las misiones existentes en la República de Bolivia—América meridional, practicada por M. R. P. Sebastián Pifferi*. Assise: Tip. de la Porciúncula.

Evans-Pritchard, Edward E. 1950. "Social Anthropology: Past and Present. The Marett Lecture." *Man* 50: 118–24.

Farré, Joseph, Françoise Martínez, and Itamar Olivares, eds. 2005. *Hommes de science et intellectuels européens en Amérique latine (XIX–XXᵉ siècles)*. Paris: Le Manuscrit.

Fausto, Carlos, and Michael Heckenberger. 2007. "Indigenous History and the History of Indians." In *Time and Memory in Indigenous Amazonia:*

Anthropological Perspectives, edited by Carlos Fausto and Michael Heckenberger, 1–43. Gainesville: University Press of Florida.

Fenchelle-Charlot, Corinne. 2014. *Jules Crevaux, l'explorateur de l'Amazonie. De la Guyane aux Andes.* Haroué: Gérard Louis éd.

Franck, Georges. 1884. *Voyages et découvertes de Jules Crevaux.* Paris: Picard et Kann.

García Jordán, Pilar. 2001. *Cruz y arado, fusiles y discursos. La construcción de los Orientes en el Perú y Bolivia, 1820–1940.* Lima: IFEA/IEP.

Giannecchini, Doroteo. 1896. *Diario de la expedición exploradora boliviana al Alto Paraguay de 1886–1887.* Asis: Tip. de la Porciúncula.

———. (1898) 1996. *Historia natural, etnografía, geografía, lingüística del Chaco boliviano.* Tarija: FIS/Centro Eclesial de Documentación.

———. 2006a. "Diario del viaje del Padre Doroteo Giannecchini, capellán castrense de la expedición terrestre al Chaco central en 1882." In *Presencia franciscana y formación intercultural en el sudeste de Bolivia según documentos del archivo franciscano de Tarija 1606–1936*, edited by Lorenzo Calzavarini, vol. 5, 583–624.

———. 2006b. "Relación de lo obrado por los Padres misioneros del colegio de Tarija en las dos expediciones fluvial y terrestre al Pilcomayo del año de 1882 [1883]." In *Presencia franciscana y formación intercultural en el sudeste de Bolivia según documentos del archivo franciscano de Tarija 1606–1936*, edited by Lorenzo Calzavarini, vol. 5, 625–666. Tarija: Centro Eclesial de Documentación.

Grandhomme, Francis. 2022. *Jules Crevaux et l'exploration de l'Amérique du Sud (1841–1882).* Paris: Les Indes Savantes.

Grieco y Bavio, Alfredo. 2016. "Ni que niño muerto: plot y pathos en los que aman, odian." Paper in *Segundas Jornadas de Literatura y Cine Policiales Argentinos: El grupo Sur, la Argentina peronista y el género policial.* Buenos Aires: Biblioteca Nacional.

Gros, Jules. 1882. "Mort du Dr. Crevaux." *Journal des voyages et des aventures de terre et de mer* XI, 298–302.

Grubb, Barbrooke W. 1919. "The Paraguayan Chaco and Its Possible Future." *The Geographical Journal* 54 (3): 151–71.

Hill, Jonathan, ed. 1988. *Rethinking History and Myth: Indigenous South American Perspectives on the Past.* Urbana: University of Illinois Press.

Holden, Edward. 1883. "The Search for Crevaux." *Science* 2 (29): 222.

Ibarreta, Juan de. 1900. *El Explorador Ibarreta en el Pilcomayo. Noticias de la prensa sud-americana acerca de la expedición.* Madrid: El Ferrol.

Jofré, Manuel Othon. (1895) 2006. "Colonias y misiones. Informes de la visita practicada por el delegado del Supremo Gobierno" [1895]. In *Presencia franciscana y formación intercultural en el sudeste de Bolivia según documentos del archivo franciscano de Tarija 1606–1936*, edited by Lorenzo Calzavarini, vol. 4, 453–533. Tarija: Centro Eclesial de Documentación.

Langer, Erick. 2009. *Expecting Pears from an Elm Tree. Franciscan Missions on the Chiriguano Frontier in the Heart of South America, 1830–1949.* Durham, NC: Duke University Press.

Le Bris, Michel. 2010. *Dictionnaire amoureux des explorateurs.* Paris: Plon.

Maire, Camille. 1982. "Centenaire. Jules Crevaux, notre concitoyen (1847–1882)." *Les Cahiers Lorrains*, 241–45.

Mendoza, Marcela. 2006. "Skulls Collected for Scalping in the Gran Chaco." In *Skull Collection, Modification, and Decoration*, edited by Michelle Bonogofsky, 113–18. Oxford: Archaeopress, BAR International Series 1539.

Métraux, Alfred. 1946. "Ethnography of the Chaco." In *Handbook of South American Indians*, vol. 1, edited by Julian Steward, 197–370. Washington, DC: Smithsonian Institution.

Ministerio de Gobierno de Bolivia. 1884. *Documentos relativos a la fundación de la Colonia Crevaux.* La Paz: Imp. de la Libertad.

Ministerio de Hacienda De Bolivia. 1883. *Esploración del Gran Chaco de Bolivia. Documentos referentes.* La Paz: Imp. de La Tribuna.

Momigliano, Arnaldo. 1993. *Ensayos de historiografía antigua y moderna.* Mexico City: Fondo de Cultura Económica.

Nordenskiöld, Erland. (1910) 2002. *La Vida de los indios. El Gran Chaco (Sudamérica).* La Paz: APCOB/Plural.

Novis, Teófilo. (1887) 2016. *El Chaco en imágenes.* Sucre: Casa de La Libertad.

———. 1917. *Los Indios del Chaco. Conférence en el Colegio Nacional Junín*, July 27, 1907. Sucre: Imp. Bolivar.

———. 1918. "Recuerdos de viajes. Expedición Crevaux," *¡Adelante!* 10.

Payeur-Didelot, Jean-François. 1899. *Trente mois au continent mystérieux.* Paris/Nancy: Berger-Levrault.

Paz Guillén, José. 1886. *A través del Gran Chaco. Relación de viaje de la expedición militar boliviana en 1883.* Buenos Aires: Imprenta Jacobo.

Pino-Díaz, Fermín del, Pascal Riviale, and Juan J. R. Villarías-Robles, eds. 2009. *Entre textos e imágenes. Representaciones antropológicas de la América indígena.* Madrid: CSIC.

Raña, Eudogio. 1882. "Informe del subprefecto de la provincia del Gran Chaco, Eudogio Raña, al prefecto de Tarija (Caiza, May 6,1882)." In Ministerio de Hacienda de Bolivia, *Esploración del Gran Chaco de Bolivia. Documentos referentes,* 44–45. La Paz: Imp. de La Tribuna.

Roldán, Natalio. 1886. "Detalles sobre la muerte del explorador Crevaux." *Revista de la Sociedad Geográfica Argentina* 4: 29–33.

Saint-Arroman, Raoul (Raoul Jolly). 1894–1896. *Les Missions françaises. Causeries géographiques.* Paris: Journal des voyages/Librairie illustrée.

Scavone Yegros, Ricardo. 2004. *Las Relaciones entre el Paraguay y Bolivia en el siglo XIX.* Asunción: Servilibros.

Sinval, Armand. 1884. *Les Pionniers de l'inconnu. Essai sur les explorateurs modernes.* Limoges: Marc Barbou & Cie imprimeurs-libraires.

Sterpin, Adriana. 1993. "La Chasse aux scalps chez les Nivaclé du Gran Chaco." *Journal de la Société des américanistes* 79 (1): 33–66.

Stewart, Charles. 2016. "Historicity and Anthropology." *Annual Review of Anthropology* 45: 79–94.

Stoler, Ann Laura. 2010. *Along the Archival Grain: Epistemic Anxieties and Colonial Common Sense.* Princeton, NJ: Princeton University Press.

Storm, Olaf. 1892. *El Río Pilcomayo y el Chaco boreal.* Buenos Aires: Cia. sudamericana de billetes de banco.

Suárez Arana, Cristián. (1916) 2007. "Apuntes históricos y geográficos." *Exploraciones,* 53–80. Santa Cruz: Fundación Nova.

Taylor, Anne-Christine. 2007. "Sick of History: Contrasting Regimes of Historicity in the Upper Amazon." In *Time and Memory in Indigenous Amazonia: Anthropological Perspectives,* edited by Carlos Fausto and Michael Heckenberger, 133–68. Gainesville FL: University Press of Florida.

Thouar, Arthur. 1884. "A la recherche des restes de la mission Crevaux." *Le Tour du Monde* 48: 209–72.

———. 1891. *Explorations dans l'Amérique du Sud.* Paris: Hachette.

———. 1906a. "Sur les bords du Pilcomayo. Les Indiens Tobas." *Journal des Voyages et des aventures de terre et de mer* 523: 22–25; 524: 43–44.

———. 1906b. "Sur les bords du Pilcomayo. Massacrés par les Tobas." *Journal des voyages et des aventures de terre et de mer* 525: 55–57; 526: 75–76.

———. 1889. "Voyage dans le Chaco boréal – 1." *Le Tour du Monde* 58: 161–206.

———. 1890. "Voyage dans le Chaco boréal – 2." *Le Tour du Monde* 59: 177–218.

Trigo, Bernardo. 1939. *Las Tejas de mi techo. Páginas de la historia de Tarija.* La Paz: Editorial Universo.

Trigo Leocadio. 1905. "El Alto Pilcomayo. Informe oficial sobre las exploraciones bolivianos." *Revista de derecho, historia y letras* 8 (23): 524–53.

———. 1914. "Informe presentado al Supremo Gobierno de Bolivia por el delegado nacional Dr. Leocadio Trigo. Expedición al Pilcomayo. Año de 1906." In *Bolivia-Paraguay*, vol. 5, 387–444, Anexos, edited by Ricardo Mujía. La Paz: Imprenta del Estado.

Vaca Guzmán, Santiago. 1880. *El Pilcomayo.* Buenos Aires: Coni.

———. 1882. *El Explorador J. Crevaux i el río Pilcomayo.* Buenos Aires: Coni.

Vaultier, Jean-Bernard. 2005. "Arthur Thouar: Le Gran Chaco, l'explorateur, l'aventurier et la Société de Géographie." In *Hommes de science et intellectuels européens en Amérique latine (XIX–XXᵉ siècles)*, edited by Joseph Farré, Françoise Martínez, and Itamar Olivares, 37–58. Paris: Le Manuscrit.

Viazzo, Pier Paolo. 2003. *Introducción a la antropología histórica.* Lima: Pontificia Universidad Católica del Perú/Instituto Italiano de Cultura.

Villar, Diego, and Isabelle Combès, eds. 2012. *Las Tierras bajas de Bolivia: Miradas históricas y antropológicas.* Santa Cruz: El País/Museo de Historia de la UAGRM.

Wagner L.-D. 1910. "Massacre de Jules Crevaux d'après les dires d'un chef Toba." *Journal de la Société des américanistes* 7 (1): 121–22.

Notes

Preface

1 Broc 1982a and 1982b.
2 Le Bris 2010: 278.
3 Known in French as "*Qui a tué Harry?*" or "Who Killed Harry?"
4 For example, *The Dogs of Riga* (2008), which, according to one blurb, "explores one man's struggle to find truth and justice in a society increasingly bereft of either; their deaths mushroom into an international incident. It is known entitled in French *Assassins sans visage*.

Introduction

1 Giannecchini (1898) 1996: 161.
2 Alfred Métraux, letter of March 9, 1928, to the Geneva Museum of Ethnography, in Aurois and Monnier 1998: 12.
3 Combès, Villar, and Lowrey 2009.
4 See, for instance, Novis (1887) 2016; Thouar 1884; Chaumeil 2009; Grandhomme 2022.
5 Borges 1996.
6 Grieco y Bavio 2016. As part of this undertaking we can mention the detective novels written by Borges and Adolfo Bioy Casares under either a real name or a pseudonym (e.g., *Seis problemas para Isidro Parodi, Un modelo para la muerte*, etc.), the short stories of Peyrou "*La Espada dormida, El Arbol de Judas*", or the novel *Los que aman, odian* by Bioy and Silvina Ocampo, as well as the collection of detective stories directed by Borges and Bioy, entitled "El séptimo círculo," which included titles by Wilkie

Collins, Nicholas Blake, John Dickson Carr, Hugh Walpole, Graham Greene, and so on.
7   Hill 1988; Fausto and Heckenberger 2007.
8   Taylor 2007.
9   Momigliano 1993; Viazzo 2003.
10 Stewart 2016; Coello de la Rosa and Dieste 2020.
11 Combès 2016.
12 Combès 2005.
13 Stoler 2010: 47.
14 Respectively, Combès 2019, 2005.
15 Evans-Pritchard 1950.

Chapter 1

1   Throughout the book, I use the term "Indian" when conveying the colonial viewpoint, since this book hinges largely on colonizer/colonized conflict.
2   *Le Courrier de la Moselle* (cited in Grandhomme 2022: 385). A reissue of Crevaux's work appeared in 1987 under the title *Le Mendiant de l'Eldorado. De Cayenne aux Andes*, 1876–1879 (Paris: Phébus).
3   *Criollo* means literally "creole." Since the term has other meanings in English, I have chosen to use the Spanish word to designate the "whites" (or mestizos) of the region, as opposed to the Indians.
4   Arthur Thouar, "Circonstances qui ont précédé et suivi le massacre de la mission Crevaux," October 5, 1899, Archives Nationales [AN], F/17/3009B, dossier Thouar, p. 2.
5   Corrado 1884: 428.
6   Tratado de paz entre los blancos de Salinas y los Tobas, 1859, Archives Franciscaines de Tarija [AFT] 1-878.
7   Report of Fr. Mauricio Monacelli (San Francisco, February 10, 1878), AFT 1-2376, f. 5v.
8   Corrado 1884: 471–73.
9   In colonial times, the Spanish called the Chiriguano leaders, and Indian leaders in general, "capitaines."
10 Letter from the Prefecture for Missions to Fr. de San Antonio (San Francisco, January 10, 1878), AFT 1-2375.
11 Campos 1888: 112–13, 123.
12 Braunstein 2006.
13 Paz Guillén 1886: 26; Campos 1888: 104.
14 Baldrich 1890: 199n1.
15 Letter from Manuel Othon Jofré to Jules Crevaux (Tarija, March 6, 1882), *El Trabajo* [Tarija], March 9, 1882, pp. 3–4.
16 Baldrich 1890: 204, 272, italics in original. See Bossert 2012.

17 Letter from Jules Crevaux to the French Minister of Public Instruction (Tarija, March 13, 1882), in Campos 1888: 618.
18 Campos 1888: 273.
19 Thouar 1891: 347.
20 Giannecchini 2006b: 645n1.
21 Giannecchini (1898) 1996: 161.
22 "Anales de este Colegio Franciscano de Tarija desde el año 1879," in Calzavarini 2006: 1251–52.
23 Corrado 1884: 436.

Chapter 2

1 B. Trigo 1939: 191.
2 Giannecchini 2006b: 639.
3 Raña 1882: 44; Letter from David Gareca to Demócrito Cabezas (Caiza, May 2, 1882), *El Trabajo*, May 11, 1882, p. 2.
4 Letter from J. Crevaux to the Bolivian Minister of Finance (San Francisco, March 17, 1882), in Ministerio de Hacienda de Bolivia 1883: 46.
5 Giannecchini 2006b: 643.
6 Gumercindo Arancibia, "Apuntes de la expedición. El cráneo de Mr. Crevaux" (Caiza, October 10, 1883), *La Estrella de Tarija*, October 24, 1883, p. 2.
7 Luis Paz, "La Exploración de Mr. Crevaux," *El Trabajo*, May 22, 1882, p. 2.
8 Giannecchini 2006b: 643.
9 In Vaca Guzmán 1882: 42–43.
10 Letter from the correspondent (Yacuiba, June 12, 1882), *El Trabajo*, July 3, 1882, p. 3.
11 Raña 1882; "Extraordinario del Gran Chaco. Fracaso de la expedición Crevaux," *El Trabajo*, May 11, 1882, p. 2; Letter sent from Caiza to Senator Bernardo Trigo, March 10, 1883, in Sinval 1884: 277–78.
12 Letter dated July 8, 1882, in Vaca Guzmán 1882: 43.
13 *El Trabajo*, May 11, 1882, p. 2.
14 Telegram from Francisco Arraya (Tupiza, May 28, 1882), published in *La Nación*, May 30, 1882.

Chapter 3

1 Letter from Fr. Vicente Marcelleti to Eudogio Raña (San Francisco, June 13, 1882), AFT 2-579; Letter from Eudogio Raña to Fr. Vicente Marcelleti (Caiza, June 18, 1882), AFT 1-2459; Letter from Fr. Doroteo Giannecchini to the Fr. warden of Tarija College (Aguairenda, July 4, 1882), *El Trabajo*, July 13, 1882, p. 3.

2   Letter from Fr. Doroteo Giannecchini to the Fr. warden of Tarija College (Aguairenda, July 4, 1882), *El Trabajo*, July 13, 1882, p. 3.

3   *La Estrella de Tarija*, July 22, 1882, p. 1.

4   Letter from Fr. Vicente Marcelleti to Fr. Doroteo Giannecchini (1882), AFT 2-617, f. 2.

5   Letter from Eudogio Raña to the Prefect of Tarija (Caiza, August 5, 1882), *El Trabajo*, August 28, 1882, p. 2; Letter from Fr. Doroteo Giannecchini to Fr. Leonardo Stazi (Villa Rodrigo [Caiza], August 6, 1882), AFT 1-898.

6   Letter from David Gareca to Demócrito Cabezas (Caiza, May 9, 1882), *El Trabajo*, May 25, 1882, p. 2.

7   Grandhomme 2022: 316–17.

8   Letter from Jules Crevaux to the Bolivian Minister of Finance (San Francisco, March 17, 1882), in Ministerio de Hacienda de Bolivia 1883: 46.

9   Luis Paz, "La Situación del Gran Chaco," *El Trabajo*, May 25, 1882, p. 2.

10   Letter from Esteban Castillo, magistrate of Ñancaroinza, to the subprefect of the Gran Chaco (May 15, 1882), Archivo y Biblioteca Nacionales de Bolivia [ABNB] Ministerior del Interior [MI] 214/17.

11   Letter from David Gareca to Doctor Demócrito Cabezas (Caiza, May 2, 1882), *El Trabajo*, May 11, 1882, p. 2.

12   Letter from Arthur Thouar to the Minister of Public Instruction, Buenos Aires, February 12, 1886, in Thouar, "Circonstances qui ont précédé et suivi le massacre de la mission Crevaux," October 5, 1899, AN, F/17/3009B, dossier Thouar, annexes.

13   Jofré (1895) 2006: 507.

14   Giannecchini 2006b: 653.

15   Thouar 1884: 230.

16   Receipt signed by the prefect of Tarija, Joaquín Lemoine (Tarija, November 27, 1882), AFT 1-902, f. 2.

17   Giannecchini 2006b: 652–53.

18   Giannecchini 2006b: 656.

19   Giannecchini 2006a: 592.

20   Giannecchini, 2006a: 607–608.

21   Paz Guillén 1886: 13; Baldrich 1890: 246; letter from Yacuiba (November 8, 1882), *El Trabajo*, November 16, 1882, p. 3; André Bresson 1886: 411.

22   Giannecchini 2006a: 616, 623.

23   Campos 1888: 41; the letter giving these objects to Thouar is found on pp. 362–63.

24   Letters from the Prefect of Tarija, Samuel Pareja, to the Minister of the Interior, July 31 and September 4, 1884, ABNB MI 221/51.

25   Baldrich 1890: 10, 21–22.

26   Roldán 1886: 29, 32.

27   Thouar 1884: 209; see Sinval 1884: 277.

28 Edward Holden 1883: 222.

29 Thouar's report to Samuel Pareja, military commander of the Paraguay (Asunción, November 17, 1883), ABNB Ministerio de la Guerra [MG] 1883 no. 25; Thouar 1884: 241.

30 Thouar 1884: 252–54.

31 Letter written from Caiza, August 12, 1883. Original French copy in AFT 2-671, p. 4.

32 Thouar 1884: 272.

33 Letter from Arthur Thouar dated May 30, 1886, cited in "Anales de este Colegio Franciscano de Tarija desde el año 1879," in Calzavarini 2006: vol 6, 1260.

34 Arancibia, "Apuntes de la expedición. El cráneo de Mr. Crevaux (Caiza, October 10, 1883)," *La Estrella de Tarija*, October 24, 1883, p. 2.

35 Campos 1888: 105.

36 Anales, 1250–51.

37 Doroteo Giannecchini, "Recuerdos de la Colonia Crevaux en 1883," AFT 1-913, f.1v.

38 Anales, 1251.

39 José M. Vargas, "Un terrible acontecimiento" (Caiza, January 15, 1884), *El Trabajo*, February 11, 1884, p. 3; letter from Fernando Soruco (Caiza, January 9, 1884), *La Estrella de Tarija*, January 15, 1884, p. 2.

40 Doroteo Giannecchini, "Recuerdos," AFT 1-913, f. 1v; my emphasis.

41 Cecilia Oviedo, "Un rescate," *El Trabajo*, July 29, 1884, p. 3.

42 Letter from Miguel Estenssoro to the Prefect of Tarija (Caiza, September 9, 1884), *La Estrella de Tarija. Diario de la tarde*, July 17, 1884, p. 2.

43 Tratado de paz, 1884, AFT 1-910.

44 Corrado 1884: 434, 439; Thouar's notes on Fr. Giannecchini, August 25, 1886, in Thouar, "Circonstances qui ont précédé et suivi le massacre de la mission Crevaux," October 5, 1899, AN, F/17/3009B, dossier Thouar, annexes, doc. 9.

45 Thouar, "Circonstances qui ont précédé et suivi le massacre de la mission Crevaux," October 5, 1899, AN, F/17/3009B, dossier Thouar, pp. 21–23.

46 *Mission E. A. Thouar. Carnet n° 1, du 26 février au 5 juin 1886.* Bibliothèque Nationale de France [BNF], Département Cartes & Plans: Archives de la Société de Géographie (Paris, Richelieu site), Ms. in-8° 12, Pièce 1266, pp. 99, 103.

47 Thouar 1889: 206–207.

48 *Primer libro de órdenes generales de la expedición Thouar*, Casa de La Libertad, Sucre [CDL], (4483), 276.

49 Paz Guillén 1886: 11.

Chapter 4

1   Jean-Pierre Chaumeil 2009: 220–21; Grandhomme 2022: 337–38.
2   Letter from Eudogio Raña to Fr. Sebastián Pifferi (Caiza, May 7, 1882), AFT 1-2455, f. 1v.
3   Letter from Eudogio Raña to Fr. Vicente Marcelleti (Caiza, July 6, 1882), AFT 1-2457.
4   Letter from Daniel Campos to Esteban Castillo (Caiza, July 23, 1883), in Campos 1888: 371–72. The author of the letter to Senator Bernardo Trigo dated March 10, 1883 says he told Campos that Iramaye might be able to provide information on Crevaux's death and the place where he was buried (in Sinval 1884: 278).
5   Letter from Fr. Romano to Fr. Giannecchini (Machareti, July 30, 1883), AFT 2-643, f. 1.
6   *La Estrella de Tarija*, July 22, 1882, p. 1.
7   Campos 1888: 35; Zeballos's appointment is annexed to the same volume, pp. 348–49.
8   Novis (1887) 2016: 10; 1918: 344. Francisco seems to have improved over the next years, since he accompanied an Argentinian expedition to the Chaco in 1903 (Asp 1905: 7); nevertheless, he made no further revelations about the Crevaux affair.
9   *Estrella de Tarija*, July 22, 1882, p. 1.
10   Luis Paz, "La Exploración de Mr. Crevaux," *El Trabajo*, May 22, 1882, p. 2.
11   Thouar, "Circonstances qui ont précédé et suivi le massacre de la mission Crevaux," October 5, 1899, AN, F/17/3009B, dossier Thouar, pp. 21–22.
12   Arthur Thouar 1906b: 75.
13   *Bulletin de la Société de Géographie de Paris* (Paris: Société de Géographie, 1884): 259; Franck 1884: 72.
14   Thouar, Arthur, Report to the Minister of Public Instruction, c. 1888, in "Circonstances qui ont précédé et suivi le massacre de la mission Crevaux," October 5, 1899, AN, F/17/3009B, dossier Thouar, annex, p. 4.
15   Letter from the Minister of Foreign Affairs and Colonization to the Chamber of Deputies (October 8, 1886), *Boletín del ministerio de Relaciones Exteriores y Colonización* 3 (1887): 7–8.
16   Anales, p. 1260; AFT 1-813.
17   David Gareca, "Lettre à Antonio Quijarro, Caiza, December 2, 1885," in Campos 1888: 710–15.
18   Campos 1888: 356, 365.
19   Interview with Thouar in the Argentinian press, republished in *El Trabajo*, January 4, 1884, pp. 1–2.
20   "Informe de la comisión informadora sobre la expedición Thouar, 1888," CDL 3-1-14, no. 886, p. 5.

21 Thouar, "Informe de la expedición al Alto Paraguay (January 30, 1888)," CDL 3-1-6, no. 906, pp. 3, 5.

22 Letter from Thouar to the Minister of Foreign Affairs (Machareti, June 3, 1887), *Boletín del ministerio de Relaciones Exteriores y Colonización* 7 (1887): 8; "Informe de la comisión informadora sobre la expedición Thouar, 1888," CDL 3-1-14, no. 886, pp. 19–20; Giannecchini 1896: 140.

23 "Informe de la comisión informadora sobre la expedición Thouar, 1888," CDL 3-1-14, no. 886, pp. 21, 25, 27.

24 Giannecchini 1896: 255.

25 Segundo libro de órdenes generales de la expedición Thouar, CDL 871: 6–7.

26 Letter from Nicolás Ortiz to the Minister of Foreign Affairs (Colonie Crevaux, August 28, 1887), *Boletín del ministerio de Relaciones Exteriores y Colonización* 7 (1887): 23–24.

27 Suárez Arana (1916) 2007: 71, 73.

28 *La Industria*, Sucre, December 1, 1887, p. 3.

29 Article published by Storm in Buenos Aires in June 1885, in Campos 1888: 702; Storm 1892.

30 Letter from Thouar to the Bolivian government, cited in Thouar, "Informe de la comisión informadora sobre la expedición Thouar, 1888," CDL 3-1-14, no. 886, p. 17.

31 "Informe de la comisión informadora sobre la expedición Thouar, 1888," CDL 3-1-14, no. 886, p. 26.

32 Thouar 1891: 417.

33 Thouar 1891: 34.

34 Thouar, "Circonstances qui ont précédé et suivi le massacre de la mission Crevaux," October 5, 1899, AN, F/17/3009B, dossier Thouar, p. 13.

35 Thouar 1891: 342.

36 Thouar 1891: 350.

37 Thouar 1891: 351, 375, 407.

38 Giannecchini 1896: 172.

39 Letter from Fr. Fernando Cosci to Fr. Pifferi (Igüembe, December 19, 1887), AFT 2-668.

40 Jean-Bernard Vaultier 2005.

41 Thouar 1891: 114.

42 Letter from Arthur Thouar to a friend (June 1885), cited in Vaultier 2005.

43 Arthur Thouar 1890: 166.

44 Thouar, "Circonstances qui ont précédé et suivi le massacre de la mission Crevaux," October 5, 1899, AN, F/17/3009B, dossier Thouar, p. 47; my emphasis.

45 Giannecchini 2006a: 583.

Chapter 5

1 Letter from Martín Barroso to Modesto Leaplaza (Yacuiba, May 12, 1882), *El Trabajo*, May 30, 1882, p. 3.
2 Letter from the correspondent (Yacuiba, June 12, 1882), *El Trabajo*, July 3, 1882, p. 3.
3 *La Estrella de Tarija*, July 22, 1882, p. 1.
4 Thouar 1884: 229.
5 Broc 1999: 104.
6 Díez Arguedas 1971: 110–11.
7 Letter from Auguste Ringel to Aniceto Valdez (San Francisco, April 19, 1882), Thouar, "Circonstances qui ont précédé et suivi le massacre de la mission Crevaux," October 5, 1899, AN, F/17/3009B, dossier Thouar, annex.
8 Campos 1888: 49; letter from Campos to the Minister of the Interior (Caiza, August 9, 1883), ABNB MI 215/32.
9 Thouar 1891: 287.
10 Letter from the Prefect of Tarija to the Prefecture Delegate Demócrito Cabezas (Tarija, March 23, 1882), *Copiador a varias autoridades desde Julio 1° de 1881 hasta el 10 de Julio de 1883*, Archivo Histórico de Tarija [AHT] 2/64.
11 Thouar 1884: 230.
12 Cutolo 1969: 405–406.
13 Barnadas 2002: 631.
14 Franck 1884: 65.
15 https://jules-crevaux.com/, consulted June 25, 2016.
16 Barbier 1899: viii.
17 AN, F17/2956A.
18 Maire 1982.
19 Payeur-Didelot 1899; Barbier 1899: viii.
20 Thouar 1891: 19–20.
21 Luis Paz, "La Exploración de Mr. Crevaux," *El Trabajo*, May 22, 1882, p. 2.
22 Paz Guillén 1886: 10; Thouar 1906b: 55.
23 Thouar 1884: 246; Campos 1888: 102; Paz Guillén 1886: 26.
24 Letter from the correspondent (Yacuiba, June 12, 1882), *El Trabajo*, July 3, 1882, p. 3.
25 Letter dated March 10, 1883 to Senator Bernardo Trigo, in Sinval 1884: 277–78.
26 Corrado 1884: 420n1.
27 Doroteo Giannecchini, "Memorial original del prefecto de misiones entre infieles del Colegio de Tarija [1885]," AFT 1-927. *Güiraita* is the Guarani name of a tree (*Bulnesia* sp.).

28 Letter from Eudogio Raña to the Prefect of Tarija (Caiza, August 5, 1882), *El Trabajo*, August 28, 1882, p. 2.
29 Testimony of Francisco Zeballos, *La Estrella de Tarija*, July 22, 1882, p. 1.
30 Paz Guillén 1886: 10; Thouar 1884: 230; 1906a: 44; Roldán 1886: 31.
31 Raña 1882: 44.
32 Letter from Eudogio Raña to Fr. Pifferi (Caiza, May 7, 1882), AFT 1-2455, f. 1v.
33 Letter dated March 10, 1883, to Senator Bernardo Trigo, in Sinval 1884: 277–78.
34 L. Trigo 1905.
35 Letter from the correspondent (Yacuiba, June 12, 1882), *El Trabajo*, July 3, 1882, p. 3; Letter from a Franciscan, June 8, 1882, in Vaca Guzmán 1882: 43.
36 Luis Paz, "La Exploración de Mr. Crevaux," *El Trabajo*, May 22, 1882, p. 2.
37 Roldán 1886: 30.
38 Letter from the correspondent (Yacuiba, June 12, 1882), *El Trabajo*, July 3, 1882, p. 3.
39 Grubb 1919: 160.
40 Letter dated June 8, 1882, in Vaca Guzmán 1882: 43. Roldán 1886: 30–31 reports the same version.
41 Luis Paz, "Más detalles sobre la muerte del Dr. Crevaux," *El Trabajo*, June 2, 1882, p. 2.
42 *El Trabajo*, July 27, 1882, p. 2; my emphasis.
43 Raña 1882: 44.
44 Letter dated June 8, 1882, in Vaca Guzmán 1882: 42; Luis Paz, "Más detalles sobre la muerte del Dr. Crevaux," *El Trabajo*, June 22, 1882, p. 22; Francisco Zeballos in *El Trabajo*, July 27, 1882, p. 2.
45 Baldrich 1890: 33.
46 L.-D. Wagner 1910: 121.
47 Roldán 1886: 30; Franck 1884: 78–79, based on a lecture given by Thouar in France. Recent publications also mention a host of Indians: "were they one thousand, two thousand?" (Fenchelle-Charlot 2014: 250). In comparison, the number of Tobas in Bolivia at the time is estimated at between 1,500 and 3,000 (Combès 2019: 177).
48 Letter from M. Milhomme (September 24, 1883), in Franck 1884: 70–71. "Aleka" is a mistranscription of *aloha*, "fermented beer," "chicha."
49 Paz Guillén 1886: 26; Baldrich 1890: 269.
50 On this theme, see Métraux 1946; Sterpin 1993; and Mendoza 2006.
51 "José Correa (December 9, 1885)," *El Trabajo*, December 22, 1885, p. 3; Felizardo is Felizardo Terceros, who questioned Iramaye in Caiza (letter dated March 10, 1883 to Bernardo Trigo, in Sinval 1884: 277–80).
52 Letter dated March 10, 1883 to Bernardo Trigo, in Sinval 1884: 277–78.

53   Roldán 1886: 31.

54   Thouar 1906b: 55.

55   Cutolo 1969: 406; Broc 1999:104.

56   Fenchelle-Charlot 2014: 253 and back cover.

57   Grandhomme 2022: 453.

Chapter 6

1   Letter from David Gareca to Demócrito Cabezas (Caiza, May 9, 1882), *El Trabajo*, March 25, 1882, p. 2.

2   Respectively: Letter from Esteban Castillo, magistrate of Ñancaroinza, to the subprefect of Gran Chaco (May 15, 1882), ABNB MI 214/17; Luis Paz, "La Exploración de Mr. Crevaux," *El Trabajo*, May 22, 1882, p. 2.

3   Letter from the correspondent (Yacuiba, June 12, 1882), *El Trabajo*, July 3, 1882, p. 3.

4   Thouar 1884: 230; Novis 1918: 343; Díez Arguedas 1971: 111.

5   Letter from Arthur Thouar to the Société de Géographie de Paris (Tacna, May 17, 1883), in Sinval 1884: 278; Thouar 1906b: 75.

6   Cutolo 1969: 406, reprinted by Barnadas 2002: 631. Lately the Friends of Jules Crevaux website, "Amis de Jules Crevaux," has made Francisco an "Indian guide": http://jules-crevaux.com/son-oeuvre/, consulted June 25, 2016.

7   Sinval 1884: 269; Gros 1882: 302.

8   This is an article devoted to Crevaux, published in 1956 in a far-right French newspaper (cited by Grandhomme 2022: 436). Fenchelle-Charlot, on the other hand, speaks of the "young Argentinian Cebellos [*sic*]," who was to serve as Crevaux's interpreter in his dealings with the Indians on the Pilcomayo (2014: 244).

9   Roldán 1886: 32.

10   Letter dated March 10, 1883, to Bernardo Trigo, in Sinval 1884: 279–80.

11   Wagner 1910: 121.

12   Letter from Fr. Doroteo Giannecchini to the Guardian of the Tarija monastery (Aguairenda, July 4, 1882), *El Trabajo*, July 13, 1882, p. 3. *N.* or *NN.* means that the writer does not know the family name.

13   *La Estrella de Tarija*, July 22, 1882, p. 1.

14   Thouar 1884: 230.

15   Letter from the Prefect of Tarija to the Minister of Finances (Tarija, July 13, 1882) *La Estrella de Tarija*, July 22, 1882, p. 2; letter from Thouar to the Société de Géographie de Paris (Tacna, May 17, 1883), in Sinval 1884: 278.

16   Letter from Eudogio Raña to Fr. Marcelleti, July 6, 1882, AFT 1-2457.

17   Letter from Elías Vacaflor to the Prefect of Tarija (San Luis, October 14, 1882), *El Trabajo*, November 9, 1882, p. 2.

18 "José Correa (December 9, 1885)," *El Trabajo*, December 22, 1885, p. 3.

19 Thouar, "Circonstances qui ont précédé et suivi le massacre de la mission Crevaux," October 5, 1899, AN, F/17/3009B, dossier Thouar, pp. 21–22.

20 Thouar 1884: 230; Novis 1918: 343.

21 Paz Guillén 1886: 11.

22 *Bulletin de la Société de Géographie de Paris*, 266.

23 Thouar 1891: 42.

24 Novis 1918: 343.

25 Baldrich 1890: 268.

26 Thouar 1906b: 75.

27 Anon. 1884: 388.

28 Théophile Novis, "Captivité chez les Indiens Matacos et Tobas. Étude des mœurs et coutumes des Indiens du Chaco. Leur civilisation possible (c. 1890)," ABNB Manuscritos (MSS) Libro 1, p. 67.

29 Thouar 1906b: 75–76. *Tumpareño peguata chirureta* means "Go with God, my friends" in Guarani. Here Thouar copies, with mistakes, the words of farewell to the explorers pronounced at the San Francisco mission by the Franciscans and their neophytes (Giannecchini 2006b: 643).

30 Wagner 1910: 122.

31 B. Trigo 1939: 178. This is apparently an isolated piece of information not mentioned in the documents gathered by Ibarreta's brother.

32 *La Tribuna*, Asunción, December 22, 1898, in Ibarreta 1900: 18.

33 *El Buenos Aires*, May 5, 1899, in Ibarreta 1900: 114.

34 Letter from Miguel Ortiz (May 6, 1899), in Ibarreta 1900: 134–35.

35 L. Trigo 1905: 525–26.

36 B. Trigo 1939: 178.

37 *El Trabajo*, June 30, 1886, p. 3.

38 Letter from Arthur Thouar to Fr. Pifferi (Sucre, July 31, 1886), AFT 1-831; letter from Thouar to Fr. Pifferi (Sucre, July 31, 1886), AFT 1-831; statements by Doroteo Giannecchini (September 13, 1886) and Sebastián Pifferi (September 7, 1886), Thouar, "Circonstances qui ont précédé et suivi le massacre de la mission Crevaux," October 5, 1899, AN, F/17/3009B, dossier Thouar, annexes.

39 Documents in annexes to Thouar, "Circonstances qui ont précédé et suivi le massacre de la mission Crevaux," October 5, 1899, AN, F/17/3009B, dossier Thouar.

Chapter 7

1 Raña 1882: 44.

2 List of the Tobas (San Antonio, January 22, 1877), AFT 2-597.

3 Paz Guillén 1886: 28; Thouar 1884: 246; Thouar 1906a: 23.

4 Segundo libro de órdenes generales de la expedición Thouar, CDL 871, pp. 28–29, 32.
5 Nordenskiöld (1910) 2002: 9.
6 L. Trigo 1905; Nordenskiöld (1910) 2002: 122.
7 *La Libertad*, Salta, December 2, 1916.
8 Ducci 1895: 20.
9 Ducci 1895: 17.
10 José Gianelli, "Relación original de las expediciones del Pilcomayo del año 1863" [s/d], AFT 2-912.
11 Giannecchini 1896: 313.
12 Corrado 1884: 404–405.
13 Letter from Fr. Vicente Marcelleti to Fr. Doroteo Giannecchini, 1882, AFT 2-617.
14 *El Trabajo*, May 18, 1882, p. 2.
15 Giannecchini 2006b: 650.
16 Letter from Eudogio Raña to the Prefect of Tarija (Caiza, August 5, 1882), *El Trabajo*, August 28, 1882, p. 2.
17 Anon. 1884.
18 *La Nación*, Buenos Aires, May 30, 1882, p. 1.
19 Cited in Sinval 1884: 269.
20 Luis Paz, "La Exploración de Mr. Crevaux," *El Trabajo*, May 22, 1882, p. 2.
21 Cited in Grandhomme 2022: 334–35.
22 Thouar 1884: 272.
23 Thouar, "Circonstances qui ont précédé et suivi le massacre de la mission Crevaux," October 5, 1899, AN, F/17/3009B, dossier Thouar, p. 19.
24 Letter from the inhabitants of Caiza to Arthur Thouar (October 18, 1887), in Thouar, "Circonstances qui ont précédé et suivi le massacre de la mission Crevaux," October 5, 1899, AN, F/17/3009B, dossier Thouar, p. 61.
25 Letter from Alexandre Lelarge (Parapeti, May 17, 1887), in Thouar, "Circonstances qui ont précédé et suivi le massacre de la mission Crevaux," October 5, 1899, AN, F/17/3009B, dossier Thouar, p. 16.
26 Thouar, "Circonstances qui ont précédé et suivi le massacre de la mission Crevaux," October 5, 1899, AN, F/17/3009B, dossier Thouar, p. 3; Novis 1918: 343.
27 Wagner 1910: 121–22.
28 Grandhomme 2022: 329.
29 Thouar, "Circonstances qui ont précédé et suivi le massacre de la mission Crevaux," October 5, 1899, AN, F/17/3009B, dossier Thouar, pp. 45–46.
30 Thouar, "Circonstances qui ont précédé et suivi le massacre de la mission Crevaux," October 5, 1899, AN, F/17/3009B, dossier Thouar, p. 42.

31 Thouar, "Circonstances qui ont précédé et suivi le massacre de la mission Crevaux," October 5, 1899, AN, F/17/3009B, dossier Thouar, p. 20.

32 Grandhomme 2022: 345; letter from Thouar to the Société de Géographie de Paris (Tacna, May 17, 1883), in Sinval 1884: 278.

33 Baldrich 1890: 259.

34 Raña 1882: 45.

35 Letter from the correspondent (Yacuiba, June 28, 1882), *El Trabajo*, July 24, 1882, p. 2; Manuel Othon Jofré, "Exploración fluvial y errestre del Gran Chaco," *El Trabajo*, May 22, 1882, p. 3.

36 Vaca Guzmán 1882: 68; L. Trigo 1914.

37 *El Tiempo*, Buenos Aires, November 3, 1899, in Ibarreta 1900: 131.

38 Cited in Grandhomme 2022: 387.

39 Raña 1882: 44.

40 Grandhomme 2022: 187–88.

41 Letter from Antonio Quijarro to Jules Crevaux (La Paz, March 9, 1882), in Campos 1888: 625.

42 Letter from Jules Crevaux to Samuel Campero (Santa Ana, March 14, 1882), *El Trabajo*, March 21, 1882, p. 2.

43 Letter from Jules Crevaux to the Minister A. Quijarro (San Francisco, March 17, 1882), in Ministerio de Hacienda de Bolivia 1883: 47.

44 In Vaca Guzmán 1882: 43.

45 Cited in Grandhomme 2022: 384.

46 *El Buenos Aires*, May 5, 1899, in Ibarreta 1900: 115.

47 Letter from Miguel Ortiz (April 27, 1899), in Ibarreta 1900: 123.

48 Ministerio de Gobierno de Bolivia 1884: 10.